Your Identity

Being Who You Are

2nd edition

Chan Smith

All Scriptures are King James Version
Definitions are from
Oxford Dictionary oxforddictionaries.com
Cover and Interior Design was done by the author.

ISBN:
ISBN 9781074837358:

DEDICATION

This book is dedicated to my loving Parents, Jeff, and Nell Smith. Their encouragement and help keep me going in the ministry. I also dedicate this book to my Grandparents, who got me started in church and taught me how to pray. I also want to dedicate this book to Mary Jane Young. She fanned the flame of revival in me and was my mentor. I owe a lot to her. She was a prayer warrior and memorized the whole Bible. She instilled in me the importance of memorizing the bible too. She was a great woman of God. Next, I want to dedicate this book to Charles Wayne Richmond, who has been there from the beginning and has the gift of wisdom. Lastly, I want to dedicate this book to Gregg Leard, who has been a great encouragement to me when I needed it the most. Without Gregg, I might not have written this book.

Contents

ACKNOWLEDGMENTS

I want to thank God for the inspiration to write this book. Without Him, I would have never been able to have the confidence to write any book or probably even be alive today. God is my all in all.

Introduction

First of all, I want to thank you for buying this book. I wrote this book for Christians worldwide to know their identity. Without knowing your identity, you can't walk in who you really are in Christ. Without it, you will not function properly, and to be honest, you will be half of what you are called to be.

I know today writing books seems to be the fad. Everyone has one out or is writing one. It seems almost that you can't be a Christian without writing one these days. Well, this book isn't indented to be just another book or a statement to say, "look at me I have a book." No, by no means. God put it in my heart when I was 13 years old to write books.

I wrote my first book at that age and sent it to Kenneth Copeland. It didn't get published because they only published ones known by him, no slam to Kenneth at all. I gave up on that due to lack of support to my ministry at that time. If I knew then what I know now about identity, then I would have gotten it published.

So, I am writing this so you will not make the same mistakes that I did in life. I pray it blesses you, and you have an encounter with God while reading it.

Chapter 1
What is Identity?

W hat is Identity, you might ask? Well, that is a good question and an excellent way to start this book. To know your identity, you need to know what identity is in the first place.

Identity is a noun. As noun is

A noun is a word that functions as the
name of some specific thing or set of things,
such as living creatures, objects, places,
actions, qualities, states of existence, or ideas.
Linguistically, a noun is a member of a large,
open part of speech whose members can occur
as the main word in the subject of a clause,

the object of a verb, or the object of a preposition.

The Definition of Identity according to the Oxford Dictionary is

NOUN
1.the fact of being who or what a person or thing is:
"he knows the identity of the bombers" ·
synonyms: name · ID · specification · identification · recognition ·
2.a close similarity or affinity:
"the initiative created an identity between the city and the suburbs"
3.mathematics
a transformation that leaves an object unchanged.
4.
mathematics

the equality of two expressions for all values of the quantities expressed by letters, or an equation expressing this, e.g., (x + 1)2 = x 2 + 2x + 1.

That is a lot of information to take in at once. So, I will put it in my own words that will last oh about 15 pages or more. I will start you out slowly with what Identity is and get into the more profound meaning at the end of this chapter. I will also list several examples so everyone can get the meaning of it.

Your identity is who you are. It's how you act and everything about you. Your identity is how you act around friends, neighbors, family, the person you are dating, or married to. It affects everything in your life, what you do, and how you do it. It's you.

When you walk down the street, believe it or not, your identity if the first thing a person sees walking past you. You might say, "hey, I don't believe that." Well, it's true.

Your identity affects how you walk, your posture, move your arms, legs, and head. A person can pick up on your identity by looking at you the first time. I know you might not believe me, but try it now. Put the book down for 30 minutes or so, get in your vehicle and go to the local store. Walk in and look at someone you don't know, now tell me if you don't get a feeling of how they are by just watching them walk. You see, people can tell it.

In grade school, one of the very first things I remember them teaching me is if you don't love yourself others will not love you. That has a form of truth in it because identity is essential.

How you think of yourself even affects your health, believe it or not. If you worry all the time, you can get sick. You might ask what does worry have to do with identity? Well, if you don't think you can take care of a situation, then you will worry about it, and worry and worry and worry until you are sick. You can lose your job, friends, and much more by worrying, to be perfectly honest to you.

Look at me; I was one of the worst worriers in the world. I worried about everything, and it made me get gray hair before my time. I have more gray hair than my father does, and worrying can cause that. I worried until God revealed to me what I am teaching you right now in the book. It changed my life, and I know it will change yours too. Now that is something to praise God about.

I worried so much at times I was crippled, yes I could walk, but I mean it was hard for me to move my legs and arms at times because of it. It would paralyze me, and that isn't a good life to live at all. I will get into that in the next chapter, but in this one, I want to focus on what is identity.

Back on the subject here, I had a rabbit trail.

I said earlier it affects how people see you even for the first time. Let me break that down for you.

The way you walk is significantly affected by your identity. If you feel you are worthless, then you will have a bent over posture and very pour walk. People can pick up on that immediately. When you sit at school, if you have a pour identity, you will slouch down in your seat so no one can see you and that will affect your back also. You will pay for that in the future if God doesn't heal it.

A person slouches over because they don't want to be seen by the public. They want to be invisible to the world. That is a person who has pour identity for one reason or the other. I know because I was one of them (next chapter). That is a horrible life to live and affects every choice you live in.

Slouching over will not make you invisible no matter how hard you try, the only thing it will do to you is make you have poor posture and other health problems. It can do the opposite, to be honest. People might see you more because of it and even give you a hard time for it. I am not saying you deserve it at all, but the bullies see it as a weakness and will exploit it.

In school, you might have an answer to a question, but you are too shy to raise your hand. You have thoughts going through your head like, what if I get it wrong, what if Johnny sees me and makes fun of me? What if the whole class laughs at me? So you sink into your chair even more while a cold shiver goes all over your body. Not a good feeling, is it? No, it isn't. Keep reading more, and you will get set free from that, God willing.

You might have a dream to be an actor, director or write movies, but if you feel you can't do that, then you never will. You might try out and freeze on the stage. That doesn't mean you don't have the talent to do it; it just means you don't have a good identity to give you the courage to do it. Yes, Identity is connected to courage.

Let's get back to how people can see your identity by looking at you. The way you dress is a part of that. You might ask how? Well, you dress the way you feel most of the time. The way you are on the inside can affect the clothes you pick. Your hairstyle is also a part of that. I am not picking on you, so don't think that. I am just trying to get you to see that identity can affect more than you know in your life.

Identity is simple, it's who you are, and it is essential to know who you are. You might say, "Chan, I know who I am." Well, you might, and you might not. Many Christians today really don't know who they are, if they did well, they would live it, to put it bluntly. Now don't judge that until you read the whole book and see what I mean by that statement.

Only part of the equation is who you are, the other part is knowing who you are, and the third part is living it.

Identity will make or break you, so to speak. I am not calling anyone a horse, but let's look at horses a little bit.

If you have a horse that competes, the horse will not jump over the fences and other obstacles if it's afraid and doesn't know he can do it. If that horse has a wrong identity, let's say, thinks he is a workhorse pulling a plow. Then he will not be able to run that course. Identity is part of the horses training and for the riders training as well.

Let's look at another example here; I will give you a few more also so you can get a picture or what I am talking about with Identity, the real you and knowing it. I want to get this across before going any farther. To have a proper identity, know what it is, and live it and to change the world. You need to know know what I am talking about.

I know people are reading this right now that are world changers. I say that a lot when I am preaching, and it just isn't a saying I say, I mean it. It has a strong effect on everyone I tell it to especially when it sinks in just like the promises in the Bible when it says to meditate on the word. It has a strong effect on people.

Confession is powerful too, but I will go into that more in another chapter and/or book ☺. You are a world changer though, but you can't be that to its fullest until you know your identity.

Next example I will give you is about a guard dog. Guard Dogs can be the best pet a person can have. They are very loyal and protective. If you have one as a family pet than they will even warn you when someone is coming to visit, or a delivery person is at the door. That comes in real handy if you can't hear because you are on the other end of the house. This isn't a book on pets but, as I said, I want you to get a clear picture of identity.

If the guard dog is scared, hasn't been trained to guard, or thinks it's a cat, then it will not be what it is. If it doesn't have a proper identity, then, in short, it isn't a guard dog, it's just a pet. I live in the country, so I know firsthand how vital guard dogs are.

Here is another example: I am sure you have watched a figure skater. Seeing how confident they are on the ice doing those scary jumps and turns. They go at high speeds then all of a sudden they stop, ON ICE, and do a twirl, (I know that isn't the technical name, but that is what it looks like to me.) Watching a figure skater can be very enjoyable, and you feel like they hear you when you scream. You feel like you are doing the figure skating yourself.

Well, that skater, they know their identity. They know they are a figure skater. How good would they do if they didn't think they were a skater? What would happen if they just got out there in the ice and didn't know they were one? Not good at all, would it? What would happen if they got scared right before that big jump? Well, they would either not do it or fall. That doesn't make for a good score. They wouldn't meet their goal of the world's top skater, would they? NO!

Now don't get me wrong here, this isn't a book about us needing to compete in life and be number one. This is a book about identity and living out our call and who God made us to be to the fullest. To be the best that we can be.

Paul said in 2 Timothy 4:7,8

2 Timothy 4:7-8King James Version (KJV)

7 I have fought a good fight, I have finished my course, I have kept the faith:

8 Henceforth there is laid up for me a crown of righteousness, which the Lord, the righteous judge, shall give me at that day: and not to me only, but unto all them also that love his appearing.

That is a robust set of verses that I often quote, and it's a good memory verse for you. Paul lived in such a way that he was happy at what he did. He was at the end of his life, and he confidently said he was ready to die, did what God wanted him to do, and lived to the fullest of his identity. That is a powerful statement to make. Not many people in the world can do that, can they?

I know some look back at their life on their death bed and are terrified at what they see. They look back in regret knowing that they could have done better. A movie plays out before them on a screen only they can see. They see the times they could have made better choices but blew it. The time they succumbed to peer pressure and took the dare. The time they took that illegal drug because Johnny said, come on do it. That one chose changed their life for the worse.

If they knew who they were, their identity, if they had a proper identity, they wouldn't have made that wrong chose. They wouldn't have felt the need to fit in, especially when the 'in' was wrong, would they? That might be you. You might be thinking about those things right now about your life. Don't worry, keep reading, you will have a chance at a better life with proper identity to make better choices for yourself and others.

Let's look at a person who has a good identity. Sally has just been picked up by her best friend, Jen. Jen takes her to a party, but Sally didn't know about it. Sally reluctantly walks in. Not long later, Johnny walks up and offers her alcohol, but she says, "no, thank you"! Johnny taunts her saying, "come on chicken drink it" and makes the chicken gesture with his arms. She says again, "no thank you" and walks off. She handled that correctly because she knew who she was. If she drank that and got drunk, she could have gotten into a wreck because her friend Jen was drunk and couldn't drive home. Sally had to drive home that night.

This isn't a book on the dangers of drinking, but I wanted to give you some more examples of how important it is to know your identity.

Let's say you are in college, and it's your turn to make a speech in front of the whole class or maybe even the entire college and the dean. Fifty percent of your class grade depends on this one speech. That is a lot of pressure there. Let me give you two scenarios to this.

Scenario one

You get up there and you freeze, you are terrified, and your notes become a blur. You look around at everyone, and thoughts go through your head like: "I can't do this, who am I?" "What was I thinking taking this class?" I am not good enough to be making this speech. Considering those things made you so scared and unworthy feeling you couldn't talk at all and made a zero. You flunked out of college! You barely make it by in life not having money at times to pay the electric bill, and at the end of your life, you look back thinking of all the times you got scared and didn't try to make more of your life.

Scenario Two

You get up to the podium and look around at all the people there waiting to hear your amazing words. Instead of freezing, you feel calm and are in complete control of yourself. Thoughts go through your head like, "I can do this; I will speak clearly and intellectually." You have confidence in yourself. You can see your notes, and it all falls in line. You make the best speech of anyone there in college. As a matter of fact, the dean says no one has given a speech like yours. In the audience was a beautiful lady that was a student there. You never saw her before and vice versa. She falls in love with you at the very first word you say. She approaches you to let you know how much she loved the speech. Your eyes meet hers, and you fall in love at first sight. You both go out to eat that day and well, you grow old together. You two have six beautiful children who become doctors, lawyers, ministers, and government. They change the world.

Not only do your children change the world, but the dean approaches you, and you get a mighty job (your dream job) and end up becoming president of the United States. You come up with ideas that haven't been thought of before. God just downloads fantastic things to you, and those ideas help create jobs for millions of people. You bring the country out of a depression.

Those two are very different outcomes. All because you have an identity and know who are you. Now, are you interested in finishing this book?

Knowing your identity not only affects you, but it will also affect your children as well as I said in the scenarios. You having a proper identity, knowing it, and walking in it affects everyone around you, especially your family. Your children will learn from you and in turn, will have a great identity and life also. I am not saying because you are born-again your children inherit that and are in turn born-again just because you are. That isn't how being born-again works, they must have their own born-again experience but knowing your identity will have a positive effect on them and in turn, they will probably get born again also.

The verse comes to mind

Proverbs 22:6 King James Version (KJV)

6 Train up a child in the way he should go: and when he is old, he will not depart from it.

You see, that is biblical proof that knowing your identity has a good effect on your children because it's an integral part in raising them correctly. If you are always scared and angry, some of the effects of not knowing your identity, then how can you expect to have a positive impact on your children's life?

That is another good reason and outcome of knowing your identity. I can give you so many examples of what I am talking about it would fill a book up and more. Like I have said before, this revelation changed my life. To me, it's the most important message for the world for everyone living right now. They need to hear this message, learn it, and live it.

Why you might ask? Well, I don't think most Christians know or grasp what the born–again experience is. It's much more than being saved from hell; it makes you a better person all around. It makes you have a better life and a better outlook! It gives you the power to see your goals. To truly understand them and do them to their fullest.

At the first of this chapter, I had the definition of Identity. I will list it again to refresh your memory.

NOUN

1.the fact of being who or what a person or thing is:
"he knows the identity of the bombers" ·
synonyms: name · ID · specification · identification ·
recognition ·
2.a close similarity or affinity:
"the initiative created an identity between the city and the
suburbs"
3.mathematics
a transformation that leaves an object unchanged.
4.
mathematics

the equality of two expressions for all
values of the quantities expressed by letters, or
an equation expressing this, e.g., $(x + 1)2 = x\,2$
$+ 2x + 1$.

I want to talk about the first two definitions and use those for the meaning of Identity. The definitions themselves are powerful, and that in itself will change your life.

"The fact of being who or what a person is," read that over to let it sink in. Being who you are. That is considered a definition of identity. I say that often in my preaching and in this book. I never knew that was a definition of identity. That is all God there, don't you love it when He does things like that? How things fall together without thinking about it. That is no coincidence; it's the Holy Spirit. He is always working behind the scenes to do even small things that often go unnoticed. Just today, writing this, I saw a person that could help me with something I need to be done. That just happened to be there and say, "I can help you with that." The Holy Spirit does those things. I just wanted to share that with you so you would know this is a divine God moment for you right now reading this.

Now back to the definitions of Identity. Being who you are. I know that might sound silly, and most of you are thinking right now reading this, "I know who I am, I am me, and I am being it." Well, most people aren't being who God made them to be. Most never see their dreams fulfilled. A lot of goals – dreams we have are God-given. Of course, the devil can corrupt that dream, but he can't create anything. Only God can create things; the devil can only corrupt or misuse what God made.

You want to be who you are, to see the dreams that God has placed inside you to its fullest, and to live the way He made you to be? Well, you can! That might sound hard, but you will find out later in this book. It's a powerful revelation and will change your life and everyone else's life forever.

Let's talk about the second definition, "*a close similarity or affinity.*" You will hear more about this in a later chapter, but being more like God is our goal, and we all should strive for that. That should be our mark to reach for. That sounds like another excellent definition for Identity, don't you agree?

Writing this chapter, God gave me an even more profound revelation of what identity is and also confirmed the message I have been preaching. I love it when God does that. He always confirms what He says. Never forget that.

Now that you know what identity is let's move on to the next chapter.

God wants great things for you, and you are a world changer.

Chapter 2
My Journey

Philippians 1:6King James Version (KJV)

6 Being confident of this very thing, that he which hath begun a good work in you will perform it until the day of Jesus Christ:

To get to know about identity and for you to get the point, I want to share with you my journey. So, you will know my struggles and problems with self-worth as a child and in adulthood. To also see how knowing my identity changed my life. Testimony is powerful, and knowing how God changed me will give you the faith to be changed to.

I was born to a young couple, just starting their journey together. My parents were very young when they had me and didn't have a lot of money. I remember when I was young, we had a wood stove for the heat that was in an old metal trailer. The trailer was very noisy in the storms. I burned my elbow on that wood stove once, and it made a scar that I had for years to come. A very painful burn, believe me! I had terrible allergies so needless to say they acted up a lot. My parents and grandparents were very loving, and they did the best they could with what they had. I also have a younger sister whom I love and look up to. I always thought she was much smarter than me and more outgoing. Don't tell her that though; I want to keep the role of mean big brother up, you know! ☺

Now I am not going much into my story because it would be a very long book in itself. I would fill a novel up with my full life story, but I wanted to share with you some marks in my life that would help you with the topic of Identity.

I went to a Middle-sized school in the country; I can remember my grandfather telling me stories about the brief school life he had as a child in Drennon Springs KY. I always loved hearing his stories and still remember them to this day. I often dream about living back then, in those times. A simple but happy life. Anyways back to my journey, from day one of Kindergarten I wasn't very popular at all. As a matter of fact, you had people that others picked on then you had me, the ones that got picked on bullied me. So, I was at the bottom of the social ladder. My school journey was filled with pain and not having good self-worth at all.

I had a praying grandmother that I love very much; she went on to be with the Lord years ago, a story in itself. Some of my earliest memories was spending time with her. I am not sure why we had a bond, but we did. Maybe it was because she had to deal with depression also, so we could relate to each other. My parents tell me stories of how, when I could first walk, would run across the road to check on my grandparents to see if they were ok. She was an amazing woman of God. My grandfather was a man that went through World War II, so nothing bothered him much. Unless he talked about the time he saw Jesus at an old church uptown. Then he would get teary-eyed that is a powerful story. Those things dropped seeds into my heart, and I feel God fall on me just typing it.

So, my life had two very different journeys at once. One, when I was with my peers I would get picked on, they would call me names, make things up to get me into trouble, so on and so forth, yes even at church around my peers, it never stopped. The other, when I was around older saints, I would feel at peace, I could relate to them for some reason and loved hearing their stories. I would take their stories in. I remember my mentor, Mary Jane Young, would teach me how to study the Bible and that has stayed with me to this day.

I felt calm around older people because I could connect with them and I was nervous, scared, etc. around the people my age because I couldn't connect. Me not being able to know my identity, not know who I was made me stick out, and my peers could smell it. They saw it all over me and took advantage of that. I don't want to say I asked for it because I didn't, but I didn't help the fact by hating who I was.

You might ask why did I hate who I was? Well, not just one thing caused that to happen, but many things all rolled up into one. That is for another time; I will go into some of it later in this chapter.

I got born again at a young age and went to church. I remember since the first; I felt Gods' presence on me in a powerful way. That started me on a journey that leads me to the place I am at now and one that I am still on. It never stops even at death for a Christian.

Being born-again and filled with the Spirit at an early age put me in a different place than my classmates. It opened me up for more persecution. For one reason, I was very prophetic at an early age, and that made me stand out. Seeing Jesus when I was around 5 or so had an impact on me, and I thought of things in the spiritual terms, and that set me apart from others. I had to learn how to deal with being different, so that affected my identity. I had no spiritual mentor that was prophetic to help me deal with being set apart like that. Mary Jane was anointed, but she wasn't very prophetic, she was a teacher. I never had that until I started studying Bill Johnson, Randy Clark, and others in the Revival Alliance that I really knew about my prophetic gift and how to use it effectively. That had a significant effect on my identity, once I knew more about the prophetic gift from people that had it.

Being prophetic though in an area that wasn't very kind to that gift or even knew about it was difficult. Now, as time went on and more people of God made sermons available via the internet things starting to change for the better. Let the prophetic arise. ☺

This isn't a book about the prophetic, but it's important to know what affected my identity throughout my life, and that is an integral part of my life. Maybe even some of you have a similar story of your life, so this might help you.

Back to my journey, I was called to minister at an early age but didn't like being in front of people due to my self-esteem. Being called to preach but not being able to stand in front of people is a huge problem to have. I also had a speech problem that was magnified because of my low self-esteem. Needless to say, I ran from my calling. I was asked to preach as part of a youth group event at the local church was in. The youth leaders noticed the call on my life to preach, so they gave me a platform to start. Well, they scheduled me and needed me to preach a long sermon due to the event length, but when I got up there, I only preached around five minutes — the shortest sermon in history, no doubt.

Preaching then was an excellent way to put my, well, maybe pinky toe in the water. I would say foot, but it was a small sermon. That did give me a little hunger for more, though.

Five years or so later, I was asked by the new Senior Pastor to preach on Wednesday night. God told me to preach on His glory. A topic I knew a lot about because I spent time in His glory at home in my room. When the pastor said my name, I stood up, and God fell on me. Well, I am sure that was the reason why I was able to preach for the length of time I did. God fell on me so strong that I couldn't be bothered by looking at the people, and the only thought in my mind was what He put there. Looking at people then made me nervous because of the fear of being in front of them.

God was on me so strong I couldn't think of anything but what He gave me and that is a good thing. No thoughts of "I am not good enough, I have a speech problem" etc. It was like God was saying, "Hey, I want to use you as a puppet for my glory." I said back to Him, "use away God, Use away."

I had notes but didn't use them, only the bible verses. I had to lean on the podium to even be able to stand up. The Pastor of the church was pinned to his seat the whole service. It was like God was saying, "it's my time to speak." God moved powerfully that night, and I preached much longer than five minutes, and that was only because God took over.

When I gave an altar call to anyone who wanted God's glory, almost everyone there that night came forward. Everyone fell down without me touching them but one older couple who was jealous. After that, some things happen among the church leadership (didn't involve me), and other things got me sick of church, and I walked away from God for years. I will go more into that later in this chapter.

I fought against God for years, and I had to go through several personal battles before I was finally willing to say yes to God's call on my life. I got back into church and started to devour God's word. I studied and let God teach me things from the word and books.

I was against grace teachings for a time then (probably had a religious spirit) but one night I was on the phone with someone, and God gave me a download.

I got freed from the religious spirit and suddenly got a revelation of what I am teaching you now in this book. That set me free from any self-doubt and fear I had. I finally knew my identity, and I have never turned back. Of course, I have times when I think, I want to get out of the ministry, but that isn't because of identity issues it is because one gets tired of battles at times.

I heard a minister say once that thinking about getting out of the ministry is normal and you probably don't have a massive call on your life if you don't think that. Well, I have an enormous call on my life then because I do believe that, but I push through it. I have learned to live just day by day and walk with God.

I had struggles with depression and discouragement for the majority of my life. It started at a very early age. The earliest moments I can remember that started my depression was when I was in Kindergarten at Trimble County High School. I had a great teacher that went on to be my principle in Elementary, and I admire her to this day. It wasn't her fault and as anyone has been around children can tell you, you can't control what they do. You merely guide them in what to do. Now that the disclaimer is out of the way, I remember being shamed and picked on by my classmates in Kindergarten.

I know that is a very early age and some might think it wouldn't have a significant effect on a person. They say you will forget it and grow out of it, but I tell you it has a considerable impact on the rest of your life. The earliest interactions you have with people groups, most of the time, will engrain an opinion of them. In my case, it engrained fear and intimidation. It also ingrained a feeling of worthlessness. I know that is going deep and making me be open, but this is important to the identity story. You need to understand how it changed my life so it can change your life to. Hey, if God can use and change me, He can use anyone as the saying goes. ☺

The experience I went through in Elementary school ended up putting me in depression that lasted until about six years ago. That is a long time.

In elementary, I had severe allergies, and I remember sneezing and got something on a girl's shirt in front of me in line for lunch. A teacher came over and was very rude to me! She made me get a towel and wipe it off the back of the girl's shirt. Of course, everyone in the cafeteria had a field day with that. I remember sitting at the table and thinking if I could get by with it, I would get under the table to eat.

A teacher named Miss Brown had a particular fondness of pointing my allergy problems out. She would regularly call me out in class and tell me I needed to blow my nose and send me out of the class. Needless to say, I frequently asked to have my mom pick me up from school early. Getting picked on and always having headaches was too much for me to go through at times. My mother is a loving mother and a very good one. I don't want to make anyone think she isn't. The things I went through wasn't her fault. She was and still is very protective of me.

One day my mother was on the way to pick me up, and someone backed into her. I remember a teacher at school shaming me for that and blaming it all on me. Folks, doing those things to a child has a profound impact on them. It's essential that we watch our words around children. Those are the most impressionable moments of their life.

Like I said earlier, at a very early age, I started attending church. I felt God on me at an early age, and that was the only place I felt at ease in public. I loved being in the presence of God so much. I never wanted to leave it. I remember going home from school at times, running to my room, crying because of my peers, but God would come down. He would love on me and help me get through those hard times.

One night I said, "God I can't live anymore like this. Take over; I give you my hands, arms, head, chest, stomach, legs, feet, and every part of my body. Take it God for your use." God fell on me so strong that night that I laid on the floor for hours not being able to move. God stayed on me for years after that all the time.

At times God was on my so strong on me people couldn't sit beside me at church because they couldn't stand His presence that strong. God would fall on them. I loved walking in His glory. I can remember several times when people had things wrong with them, and without me praying they would get healed.

Let me give you three examples of healing I saw at a young age.

My grandparents took me to church every time the doors opened. We would always bring a neighbor with us that came to our church. She was and still if a very anointed lady that God uses. Anyways, she had this massive place on the back of her neck. Now I could only get by with this because I was very young so I am not saying it's ok for grown men to do this and I probably wouldn't do this again. I was sitting next to her in the back seat of my grandparent's car as we set in the parking lot of the Country Store. My grandfather was inside shopping. We were coming home from church, and that was a routine stop for us. She told me about the place, and I looked at her and just took my hand and grabbed the spot on her neck with no warning. Well, the spot left her neck and to my knowledge has never come back all these years later. That was a powerful experience. I didn't even say a word or even pray. I just said it's gone now when grabbing it.

It says to heal the sick not pray for them by the way, that verse is in Matthew 10:8. That teaching is for another book. ☺ Sorry

Matthew 10:8King James Version (KJV)

8 Heal the sick, cleanse the lepers, raise the dead, cast out devils: freely ye have received, freely give.

The next story I will share with you is about a man's legs being grown out.

This story also happened when I was young, as did the next one. At the church I grew up in we had a healing class. It was to teach people how to flow in the gift of healing. Ray Meadows taught it, and I was the only young person there. I couldn't get enough of God and His word. I wanted to learn all I could. One class they taught us about was that people having back trouble might have one leg shorter than the other.

Brother Meadows put us in pairs and told the other one to sit down in a chair. I was paired with Ira Glen; I remember this as if it happened today. I knelt and raised his legs up and noticed one was a lot shorter than the other, and without me speaking a word, it grew out to be longer than the other. It was growing and growing and needless to say, I was freaking out. I panicked! I thought I just injured him for life, and I thought my short life in the ministry was over. I screamed out to Brother Ray saying, "What do I do know, I just raised Brother Ira's legs up, and the shorter one started growing, and now it's longer! I didn't even say a word; it just started growing!" Brother Ray was a very wise man, and without him, I might not have the healing anointing on my life today. Brother Ray said, "Chan, command it to stop growing and tell the other one to grow out to match it, then stop!" So, I did, and you know what, in front of my eyes, Ira grew at least an inch. I have no idea why Brother Ray said to command the other one to grow out and not for the once shorter leg to shrink to the same length as the other.

All I know is that was what happened that day at church. Maybe it was God saying, "Once I bless you, I will not take it back no matter what."

The last example I will give is about a healing of a place on someone's legs.

One day I rode with my grandmother uptown, and we stopped at the apartments where a cousin of mine lived. I wasn't 16, yet so I couldn't drive. When I turned 16 and got my driver's license, I did a lot of driving for them and loved doing it. My grandmother had one eye missing, so it was hard for her to see, especially when she got older. I loved my grandparents dearly, and driving for them gave me another chance to spend time with them. I loved spending time with them.

My grandmother had a significant impact on my life, and I wouldn't be a pastor today if it weren't for her influence. She was a praying woman and often prayed that I would become a great minister one day. I don't know if I am great, but I am a minister, so at least part of that prayer happened. ☺

Back to the story, my grandmother and I were at the Bedford Apartments talking to my cousin. She said she had a place on her leg that hurt. The power of God was on me, and I looked at her with faith. I told her, "No, you don't; the pain is gone." I said it in faith, knowing that without a doubt, God took it away. She looked at me and said, "you know what, you are right; it's gone."

Things like that happened regularly to me, and it wasn't because I was something special. It was because God is something special and He loves me like I am something special like He does us all! I can go into a story after story about how God moved in my life. Let me give you a few more stories.

When I was young, we lived in an old trailer that had a metal roof. My bedroom was at one end of the house, and my parents were on the other end. The light switch didn't work to turn on the lights in my bedroom, well except for me. When I turned it on I would say "in the name of Jesus turn on," and the switch would work. I was the only person it would work for. I didn't want it fixed because that would mean I wouldn't be the only one that would be able to come into my room. ☺ Win Win for me.

Another story about when we lived in the old trailer happen at night. Every night, I would walk to my parent's room at the other end of the house. I was young, and this was before my sister was born, so I was probably 5 or younger. One night, as usual, I was walking to their room. We had a front door that had a vinyl floor area in front of it with one end rounded, then regular carpet on the living room floor. I got to the front door, turned, then looked and standing right there in front of the door was Jesus. I know now it was Jesus, but then I didn't know what the being was. It was glowing light and just stood there. I screamed with everything in me because I was very young and didn't know what was going on — a typical reaction from a 5-year-old. My mom immediately came and only got to the door of her bedroom. She saw the same thing I did and felt it, but it quickly disappeared.

That marked my life, and I will never forget that moment for the rest of my life. It was like God was saying, "I have marked you for my work and have a call on your life." That dropped a hunger in me for more of

God and to know Him. The hunger is still with me even to this day. I remember telling people about that experience at an early age, and I still tell people about it. I feel God just thinking about it. I can see it in my mind right now just typing this like it was happening now, at this moment. That is pretty good considering that was years ago.

I have had several experiences similar to that in my life. My childhood was marked with encounters with God and being close to Him. However, it was also marked with depression and being bullied at school. Two very different things were going on at the same time. That is why it's so important to have a proper identity.

For one reason, knowing your identity will help when you are bullied so that you can push that to the side and not let it affect you as a person. Of course, it will still bother you, but you don't have to let it determine who you are and hinder you from having a good life. I wasn't wholly freed from that until I was an adult, and God gave me the revelation of who I was and how He saw me.

Don't get me wrong; God loved on me when I was a child, and throughout my teenage years. Like I said at times, God was on me so intense I felt like I was going to die. When I say at times, I mean a lot. God was overshadowing me and walking with me. Someone gave me wrong advice though about God being on me to a point I couldn't handle it. They said to ask God to not be so strong on me. I mistakenly took that advice and asked Him to remove some of His presence from me. Well, that was probably the worst mistake of my life that I spent years dealing with the consequences.

Deep down, I might have taken that advice because I mistakenly felt I wasn't good enough. That I didn't deserve His presence like that and someone else should feel that and not me. That I was just a dumb country boy that had a speech problem and God couldn't use me. I know that is a massive contrast to the huge things I saw God do through me, but that was going on all at the same time. Today, I now know that I should have prayed my favorite prayer, "**More Lord, even if it kills me!**"

You might ask how could that happen both at the same time? Well, the bible does talk about spiritual warfare. The devil didn't like what was happening in my life, and he was doing everything he could to stop it. Without proper teaching, the devil had a hay day with me. I am sorry to say I let him. I am thankful God never gave up on me.

Another story that comes to me now is when I was very young and living in Oklahoma. My parents moved there with several relatives and friends. Most of them worked at an oil rig there. It wasn't a great living, but it paid the bills. I remember dad telling me stories about the times he had there. I was too young to remember most, but this one I do remember very clearly.

We lived in what was called tornado alley. Tornados happen regularly there without any notice at times because the weather radars weren't as advanced as they are now. We just got home and was about ready to open the door on the R.V. we lived in. Immediately a tornado struck and lifted the R.V. into the air and landed it back down. The R.V. kept doing that, so we ran back to dad's truck. I know God was there because it never touched the truck. A cousin of mine was in the military, and he was helping get everyone to safety. Some teenagers were in a trailer, and the tornado turned it over burring them alive! He was trying to dig them up and would walk over to our truck to keep us up to date. The whole time I was on the floorboard of the truck. Hey, I was young and scared! ☺

We moved around a little for a while with other relatives, and I attend a few schools. My sister wasn't born yet, so she didn't have those experiences. I do remember that we as a family was very close those years. We all depended on each other. There was no internet or cable time back then. We just had very few channels if any so entertainment, for the most part, was family oriented. The adults would play cards, and the children would play make-believe. We had good imaginations.

We didn't spend a lot of years on the road, but it did have a significant impact on me to this day. I am not saying that hurt me and caused me to have depression because it didn't. To be honest, moving around helped me to a degree. It was when we went back home to Kentucky was when the trouble started back up for me. Very strange, I know. I have heard ministers say, and this does seem to be accurate, that where God has called you to be, you will have the most opposition. The devil doesn't want you to succeed in that area. He wants you to give up.

Perseverance is a huge part of doing anything for the Lord. When things get hard, you can't give up and throw in the towel. You have to hang in there, and if you can't move forward, the Bible says just to stand.

Ephesians 6:10-18King James Version (KJV)

10 Finally, my brethren, be strong in the Lord, and in the power of his might.

11 Put on the whole armour of God, that ye may be able to stand against the wiles of the devil.

12 For we wrestle not against flesh and blood, but against principalities, against powers, against the rulers of the darkness of this world, against spiritual wickedness in high places.

13 Wherefore take unto you the whole armour of God, that ye may be able to withstand in the evil day, and having done all, to stand.

14 Stand therefore, having your loins girt about with truth, and having on the breastplate of righteousness;

15 And your feet shod with the preparation of the gospel of peace;

16 Above all, taking the shield of faith, wherewith ye shall be able to quench all the fiery darts of the wicked.

17 And take the helmet of salvation, and the sword of the Spirit, which is the word of God:

18 Praying always with all prayer and supplication in the Spirit, and watching thereunto with all perseverance and supplication for all saints;

We can't forget that powerful set of verses, especially when things go hard. I know that now, but it was hard for me when I was younger. I am thankful that I have grown more mature in the Lord. We must be able to have the maturity to handle the glory of God on our lives, or it could easily be our undoing too. You might ask why? Well, let's look at another verse.

Luke 12:48King James Version (KJV)

48 But he that knew not, and did commit things worthy of stripes, shall be beaten with few stripes. For unto whomsoever much is given, of him shall be much required: and to whom men have committed much, of him they will ask the more.

I do not want that to scare anyone away from the things of God. By no means do I want that. I want to get the point across that just because God touched you doesn't mean you should run off and start a ministry on your own without being mature in the Lord. Grow in the Lord and have godly people around you. It does say in the bible the following.

Proverbs 11:14King James Version (KJV)

14 Where no counsel is, the people fall: but in the multitude of counsellors there is safety.

You will find out even when you're mature you should always have people around you to help you, to hold your arms up. Moses even had to have that.

Exodus 17:12King James Version (KJV)

12 But Moses hands were heavy; and they took a stone, and put it under him, and he sat thereon; and Aaron and Hur stayed up his hands, the one on the one side, and the other on the other side; and his hands were steady until the going down of the sun.

I was always cautious about not just going out on my own and starting anything. I am currently the founder, and Senior Pastor of Revival is Here Church, but I still rely on people. Even now, I would never even think about being a lone wolf, just building my own things. That isn't in the bible at all. That is a downfall of many churches and ministries today, people getting a touch and just running off on their own — more about that in a later chapter or book.

When I was younger, God put on my heart to write books, papers, and other Christian things to share what God put on my heart. I had the blessing of many over me, so I wrote a small book about the gospel but never got it published. I even started Chan Smith Ministries, but I never gave myself a title. I just wanted to do God's work. God was always on me like I said before, and I had it in my mind I would bring revival to America. I knew God had something huge in store for this country, and I wanted to be a part of it. God started telling me about revival, more about that later, even before it was fashionable or even said.

I loved God's presence, and I thought the church in America would too. I started telling everyone a revival was coming. God was going to show up in power and bring in a harvest. That quickly became all of my thoughts. I would pray for revival in all my free time. Finally, revival was starting to be talked about in the churches again. It wasn't a closet conversation anymore. I am not for sure if I had anything to do with it or not, and it didn't matter to me. I was just happy it was talked about. I finally started to see God moving in places around the world via a Christian magazine and a Christian TV channel.

I couldn't get enough of it, as soon as the magazine would come in, I would rush to my room and read it. My young heart would be filled with the fire of God as I read the testimonies. I thought maybe this is it; maybe this is the big revival God told me about. I found out later that was just a small wave.

In the area, I lived in hunger for revival wasn't that powerful. Yes, a few here and there would get excited about it, but for the most part, people just wanted the same old same old in the church. They were happy with their sweet songs and short sermons and then went home. Yes, God would show up from time to time in a few churches, when I say time to time I mean one service or two here and there. God showing up wasn't a regular thing as it was in the bible. I felt a longing for something more in a service. I wanted and thought everyone should feel God like I did. I also thought it should be in the open in the main service, not just in my bedroom. God should be able to move outside of the closet, but it seemed some were happy for just the closet move of God.

When I read the bible, I saw God showing up clearly, out in the open. God moving was a regular thing, even in the early church. You see Him move in the following verses in the bible. They're some of my favorite verses to read.

Acts 2:1-8King James Version (KJV)

2 And when the day of Pentecost was fully come, they were all with one accord in one place.

2 And suddenly there came a sound from heaven as of a rushing mighty wind, and it filled all the house where they were sitting.

3 And there appeared unto them cloven tongues like as of fire, and it sat upon each of them.

4 And they were all filled with the Holy Ghost, and began to speak with other tongues, as the Spirit gave them utterance.

5 And there were dwelling at Jerusalem Jews, devout men, out of every nation under heaven.

6 Now when this was noised abroad, the multitude came together, and were confounded, because that every man heard them speak in his own language.

7 And they were all amazed and marvelled, saying one to another, Behold, are not all these which speak Galilaeans?

8 And how hear we every man in our own tongue, wherein we were born?

Acts 4:31King James Version (KJV)

31 And when they had prayed, the place was shaken where they were assembled together; and they were all filled with the Holy Ghost, and they spake the word of God with boldness.

Acts 10:34-48King James Version (KJV)

34 Then Peter opened his mouth, and said, Of a truth I perceive that God is no respecter of persons:

35 But in every nation he that feareth him, and worketh righteousness, is accepted with him.

36 The word which God sent unto the children of Israel, preaching peace by Jesus Christ: (he is Lord of all:)

37 That word, I say, ye know, which was published throughout all Judaea, and began from Galilee, after the baptism which John preached;

38 How God anointed Jesus of Nazareth with the Holy Ghost and with power: who went about doing good, and healing all that were oppressed of the devil; for God was with him.

39 And we are witnesses of all things which he did both in the land of the Jews, and in Jerusalem; whom they slew and hanged on a tree:

40 Him God raised up the third day, and shewed him openly;

41 Not to all the people, but unto witnesses chosen before God, even to us, who did eat and drink with him after he rose from the dead.

42 And he commanded us to preach unto the people, and to testify that it is he which was ordained of God to be the Judge of quick and dead.

43 To him give all the prophets witness, that through his name whosoever believeth in him shall receive remission of sins.

44 While Peter yet spake these words, the Holy Ghost fell on all them which heard the word.

45 And they of the circumcision which believed were astonished, as many as came with Peter, because that on the Gentiles also was poured out the gift of the Holy Ghost.

46 For they heard them speak with tongues, and magnify God. Then answered Peter,

47 Can any man forbid water, that these should not be baptized, which have received the Holy Ghost as well as we?

48 And he commanded them to be baptized in the name of the Lord. Then prayed they him to tarry certain days.

When I read those verses and saw how God should move, I wondered why I didn't see it regularly as it should be. I knew in my heart there was more of God to be had. Maybe I just wasn't ready and had to go through more in life to get to a place to see more of Him. To get rid of the depression I had in my life.

I wasn't for sure why I had to deal with depression. Was that my thorn in the flesh liked Paul had.

2 Corinthians 12:7King James Version (KJV)

7 And lest I should be exalted above measure through the abundance of the revelations, there was given to me a thorn in the flesh, the messenger of Satan to buffet me, lest I should be exalted above

I know now that the above verse was talking about a person coming against Paul and not a personal issue. I did have several of those though and always have. That will always happen to those who are on the cutting edge of what God is doing. If a person is mature, it will not bother or hold a person back. I am not saying it should happen, but it does. You would think the church had matured over the last two thousand years, at least in some ways, wouldn't you?

Getting back to my journey with identity. In middle school, I still had to go through the bullying, but it was worse. There were more chances to be alone because of class changes, and they took advantage of it believe you me. I remember getting in an argument with one of my teachers, she was an atheist, and I was a believer. She wanted to know how the world was made, and I told her I understood. I began to recite her bible verses. I know now that a person needs to depend on the Holy Spirit for words in those times and not one's mind. I can't convict anyone only Jesus and debating is clearly preached against in the bible.

Titus 3:9King James Version (KJV)

9 But avoid foolish questions, and genealogies, and contentions, and strivings about the law; for they are unprofitable and vain.

I am glad God is patient with us. He gives us plenty of time to learn and go with Him. He never gives up on us, and I am living proof of that. I do think though that sometimes we push more people away from God than pull to Him by our debating what the bible says. No one wins in debating, and like I said, only the Holy Spirit can draw someone anyways.

John 6:44King James Version (KJV)

44 No man can come to me, except the Father which hath sent me draw him: and I will raise him up at the last day.

John 16:13-14King James Version (KJV)

13 Howbeit when he, the Spirit of truth, is come, he will guide you into all truth: for he shall not speak of himself; but whatsoever he shall hear, that shall he speak: and he will shew you things to come.

14 He shall glorify me: for he shall receive of mine, and shall shew it unto you.

John 15:26King James Version (KJV)

26 But when the Comforter is come, whom I will send unto you from the Father, even the Spirit of truth, which proceedeth from the Father, he shall testify of me:
1 John 5:6King James Version (KJV)

6 This is he that came by water and blood, even Jesus Christ; not by water only, but by water and blood. And it is the Spirit that beareth witness, because the Spirit is truth.

I remember middle school being filled with running to the next class to stay away from bullies. It was an everyday thing for someone to say something demeaning to me to get a rise out of others and me. Gym class was particularly adventurous because in good weather we had to go outside.

One instance we were playing volleyball outside on a beautiful sunny day. The wind was blowing, and it felt wonderful. I was wearing sweat pants because I never wore shorts. I don't know why, but I just never felt comfortable wearing shorts in public. I felt like I was naked and needed more clothes on. Maybe it was because me being raised in church but I don't recall them ever preaching it was wrong to wear shorts. It was either a personal thing or a spiritual thing that God only put in my heart. Now that I recall, I don't remember any of the males in my family wearing shorts, so it was probably a country thing. Now, I am not saying it is wrong for anyone to wear shorts at any time. I am just saying for me personally. Sometimes we make personal convictions mandatory for everyone!

Now back to the story, I was outside in gym class on a lovely sunny, windy day. The weather was perfect, and it couldn't have been better. Perfect day to be out if I wasn't in school. A couple of boys came up to me, and one got a handful of sand. He looked at me with that mean look on his face and threw the sand in my hair.

When I was younger, I had very dark, very thick hair. They bullied me by calling me Elvis because of my thick dark hair. I hated being called that even though I didn't hate Elvis. I hated it because it wasn't a compliment to them, they meant it as a putdown, and I knew it. They would laugh at me and say, "Hey, Elvis." It made me want to shave my head, and I guess that was one thing that made me have depression and hate my personal appearance.

When the boy threw the sand in my hair, because it was thick and oily, the sand became like concrete. It was horrible, and I couldn't wait to get home that day believe me. I had a tough time getting it out, and after that, I always stayed to myself, especially in the gym. The gym class was downstairs and sort of by itself, so it made it an easy place to get bullied.

After that incident, I always campaigned to make gym just an elective and not mandatory. Maybe one day it can be. It's good to have good health, but it can open children up to being bullied for whatever handicap they have. I am not a politics person, just writing from my personal experience. I am not sure what gym can do for a person in the long run in terms of training them for adulthood unless they want to be a professional athlete. Okay, my rant is over.

Several more traumatizing things happened in Middle school, but those are the only ones I will list now. I always noticed though that the more bullying I went through in or out of church, the more the glory of God would rest on me. I am not sure if there is a significant correlation with that or not, but in the Bible, they did get persecuted. Jesus said in the following verse

John 15:17-21King James Version (KJV)

17 These things I command you, that ye love one another.

18 If the world hate you, ye know that it hated me before it hated you.

19 If ye were of the world, the world would love his own: but because ye are not of the world, but I have chosen you out of the world, therefore the world hateth you.

20 Remember the word that I said unto you, The servant is not greater than his lord. If they have persecuted me, they will also persecute you; if they have kept my saying, they will keep yours also.

21 But all these things will they do unto you for my name's sake, because they know not him that sent me.

Paul says that it can't separate us from God though in the following verse.

Romans 8:35King James Version (KJV)

35 Who shall separate us from the love of Christ? shall tribulation, or distress, or persecution, or famine, or nakedness, or peril, or sword?

Praise God for that, or we all would be in trouble. I am sure everyone reading this has had their own trials to go through in their lifetime. I am sure I am not the only one, and some of you have gone through much worse than me. The worst of the persecution hasn't been written yet; just keep reading I will get to it.

The reason why I am writing my journey in this book isn't to have a pity party or for me to get famous. My goal and purpose are to fully convey what identity is and how it can change your life, knowing it fully. By reading what I went through, the struggles I had, and how God helps me overcome them, you too can overcome. Testimonies are powerful believe me, and they are prophesy also.

Revelation 19:10King James Version (KJV)

10 And I fell at his feet to worship him. And he said unto me, See thou do it not: I am thy fellowservant, and of thy brethren that have the testimony of Jesus: worship God: for the testimony of Jesus is the spirit of prophecy.

Here are some verses talking about Paul's persecutions.

Acts 9:29King James Version (KJV)

29 And he spake boldly in the name of the Lord Jesus, and disputed against the Grecians: but they went about to slay him.

Acts 13:50King James Version (KJV)

50 But the Jews stirred up the devout and honourable women, and the chief men of the city, and raised persecution against Paul and Barnabas, and expelled them out of their coasts.

Acts 14:5King James Version (KJV)

5 And when there was an assault made both of the Gentiles, and also of the Jews with their rulers, to use them despitefully, and to stone them,

Acts 14:19King James Version (KJV)

19 And there came thither certain Jews from Antioch and Iconium, who persuaded the people, and having stoned Paul, drew him out of the city, supposing he had been dead.

Acts 16:22King James Version (KJV)

22 And the multitude rose up together against them: and the magistrates rent off their clothes, and commanded to beat them.

Acts 18:12King James Version (KJV)

12 And when Gallio was the deputy of Achaia, the Jews made insurrection with one accord against Paul, and brought him to the judgment seat,

Acts 21:36King James Version (KJV)

36 For the multitude of the people followed after, crying, Away with him.

Acts 22:22King James Version (KJV)

22 And they gave him audience unto this word, and then lifted up their voices, and said, Away with such a fellow from the earth: for it is not fit that he should live.

Acts 23:10King James Version (KJV)

10 And when there arose a great dissension, the chief captain, fearing lest Paul should have been pulled in pieces of them, commanded the soldiers to go down, and to take him by force from among them, and to bring him into the castle.

1 Corinthians 4:12King James Version (KJV)

12 And labour, working with our own hands: being reviled, we bless; being persecuted, we suffer it:

2 Corinthians 4:9King James Version (KJV)

9 Persecuted, but not forsaken; cast down, but not destroyed;

2 Corinthians 11:24King James Version (KJV)

24 Of the Jews five times received I forty stripes save one.

2 Timothy 2:9King James Version (KJV)

9 Wherein I suffer trouble, as an evil doer, even unto bonds; but the word of God is not bound.

2 Timothy 3:11King James Version (KJV)

11 Persecutions, afflictions, which came unto me at Antioch, at Iconium, at Lystra; what persecutions I endured: but out of them all the Lord delivered me.

The following verse I always had a hard time with. I am not saying it isn't from God, but I had a hard time living this verse until recently. It's a lot to swallow, so to speak, and shows if someone is mature in the Lord.

2 Corinthians 12:10King James Version (KJV)

10 Therefore I take pleasure in infirmities, in reproaches, in necessities, in persecutions, in distresses for Christ's sake: for when I am weak, then am I strong.

That is a loaded verse to read and putting it into actions is hard for any person, so please don't beat yourself up if you have a hard time with it. It only comes in time. I connect that verse with the following.

Romans 5:2-5King James Version (KJV)

2 By whom also we have access by faith into this grace wherein we stand, and rejoice in hope of the glory of God.

3 And not only so, but we glory in tribulations also: knowing that tribulation worketh patience;

4 And patience, experience; and experience, hope:

5 And hope maketh not ashamed; because the love of God is shed abroad in our hearts by the Holy Ghost which is given unto us.

As you can see, patience only comes through several tribulations and trails. It even implies that taking pleasure and glory in them only comes with having gone through several. I know that is a loaded statement, so I want to clarify it before we go on.

I am not saying we have to go to through trials and tribulations to get into heaven or be a Christian. I am also not saying we have to go through them even, but as part of living in this world, every one of us probably will go through them, especially if you are or will do anything for the Lord. It's just a matter of fact. I am sure everyone reading this book has gone through something in their life one time or another. Some have gone through more than others. That is a sad and a terrible fact of life and the world we live in today.

A verse comes to mind that has always helped me go through things, and I know it will help you.

Romans 8:28King James Version (KJV)

28 And we know that all things work together for good to them that love God, to them who are the called according to his purpose.

That is a powerful verse and something to meditate on. What the devil has meant for evil, God will turn around for the good. That is something to shout about. I know I do all the time and probably always will shout about it even in heaven.

Now let's get back to my journey. I covered some of the things that happen to me in middle school, so now let's review some things that happened to me in high school. The worst trauma in my early life occurred there. For one thing, I took a car repair class one semester, which turned out to be the worst mistake of my high school life.

Trimble County High School offered some students a chance to take free vocational classes in the first part of the day. When getting to school, we would load on a bus and travel to Carrollton, KY. to a special vocational school building. I don't recall if adults were allowed to take the classes or not, but I do know the class I was in only had male students from high school. I took car repair, but some of the other classes offered were starting businesses, wielding, electrical, and nursing. It was an excellent opportunity for students don't get me wrong. It prepared people for the world and gave them some basic training for a career they wanted to go into as an adult. I don't want to imply that the school was terrible, it wasn't. Just my experience was awful. The school handled it very well, all but the teacher I had.

I am still not sure why I took the class. I never wanted to work on cars as even a hobby. Maybe it was because I wanted to learn how to work on my car to save on repair bills. What happened traumatized me so much I was never able to work on them afterward. I never even changed the oil in a vehicle after that.

My school day would be me driving my old car to school, that I proudly paid for myself. I had two different cars as a teenager; one was a Ford Tempo I bought from my grandparents. My grandmother's sister gave it to her as a present, and I wanted it bad. It was my first car and a good one. The other one was a rusty grey, Chevy Cavalier that idled too high. When putting it into gear, the car would jump forward an inch or so. It got me from point a to point b though, even in the worst snow storm up to that time. I will share that story with you a bit later. I bought the grey cavalier from the Bedford Bank; they repossessed it.

When I got to school, I would load a bus to the Carrolton vocational school to attend car repair. The students in the class didn't respect me at all and took every chance to let me know it even on the ride there. I remember several times wanting to cry when I was riding back to Trimble County High School. It was a horrible semester. Let me tell you. After that, I never took any more classes at the vocational school or any vocational school for that matter.

One day when I got to the car repair class, the teacher left us students to take care of ourselves. He often did that for some reason or another. My classmates all got together and raised the trunk of a car. They got a chain and duct tape out and grabbed me. They proceeded to put my hands together like I was going to get handcuffed then wrapped my hands in duct tape several times and put a chain around me. I could hear them laughing and screaming while they were doing it. It was the highlight of their day but the worst time of my life.

All of a sudden, I felt God strongly fall on me. What I did afterward had to be God, and even the students said so. I blacked out, and after I came to, they told me I broke the duct tape and got the chain off me. Now if anyone knows duck-tape, they know it's very hard to impossible to break like that especially by a human. I wasn't that large back then, especially compared to the other students. I forgot to tell you that they were all holding me when I had the chain and duct tape on. They told me I pushed them all down to the ground and almost broke one boy's arm. All I know is when I came to I was standing and they were on the ground. I know at least one boy that day knew God was real, and I think he turned his life over to Him. Do you want to know why they raised the trunk of the car? They were going to put me in it, but as you can see, that didn't happen. God took over. Praise God for that. They confessed to it all and was dealt with accordingly.

I am not condoning violence in any form what so ever. Please don't get that by reading what happened to me. You can be put in situations at times when the only thing you can do is protect yourself like that. God knew I didn't have it in me to harm someone even if it was to save my life, so He took over. I knew after that how Samson in the bible could do what He did.

Judges 16:30King James Version (KJV)

30 And Samson said, Let me die with the Philistines. And he bowed himself with all his might; and the house fell upon the lords, and upon all the people that were therein. So the dead which he slew at his death were more than they which he slew in his life.

The only way Samson could do the things he did was if God fell on him. The feats he did wasn't humanly possible to do on their own. He pushed a building down with just his hands. Samson was also older at that time. The bible verse comes to mind.

Matthew 19:26King James Version (KJV)

26 But Jesus beheld them, and said unto them, With men this is impossible; but with God all things are possible.

That verse was true with Samson and with me too. God knew the only way for us to deal with the situation we went through was to take over and give us supernatural strength that only comes from Him. I want to thank God He did because if He didn't, I probably wouldn't be writing this book today. I wouldn't be alive without the supernatural strength from God.

God healed me from the trauma of that experience, though when I got the revelation, this book is about. Keep reading, and I know you will get healed from things too.

My high school years were filled with being bullied, similar to the event that happened at the vocational school. I was so happy when I graduated high school to get free from all the bullying I received. I haven't run into any of the bullies from the car repair class after I graduated, and I am not sure what happened to them. I pray they repented and got freed from bullying others.

Before I move on though I promised I would tell you about the snow storm. One day I had to work in La Grange at Kroger's. I was 16 at the time and didn't have any driving experience in winter weather. It was winter, and I didn't get to watch the weather to see if it was going to storm that day. I was working in the back, and when it was time to get off work, I walked to the door and noticed something horrible. Over an inch of solid ice was covering everything. I mean everything. It was dark and already passed the freezing point so the roads wouldn't get any better that night.

I finally got my car deiced and warmed up; I turned the C. B. radio on in the car, it came with it, the only fully working thing in the car. I heard a semi-truck driver come over the radio and say, "I am on the hill on I-71 south and can't get up it. I am right before the Pendleton exit." That made me fearful all the way to my bones. I was scared to death as the saying goes.

I started praying and took off on the way home. Oh, I forget to tell you this was way before the Cellphone days too. So, no calling home to get help or say I am on my way.

I drove very slowly, almost a crawl. I prayed all the way home with my whipper blades working full time. It was terrifying to drive home, but I did make it. I was praising God when I pulled in the driveway. I learned how to drive in winter weather that day, glad it wasn't a crash course though. Get it? I called in the next day for the whole week, and all the interstates were closed for the week also. It was a record-breaking storm.

After graduation, the church I attended was going good until a series of events happened. To this day, I am not sure what happened because I tried to stay out of the business of the church and focus on God. I could get by with that being that I was a teenager. I don't want to go into all that happened in church because I don't want to, and being it didn't have anything to do with me, I will stay out of it.

I said earlier, "I was close to my grandmother," and I was there before she died. She sang hymns and was praising God. It was glorious to see let me tell you. That helped with dealing with her passing away, but it still bothered me greatly.

After her passing, because of the stuff happening in church (I am not blaming the senior pastor and founder at all) and being bullied, I started to lose interest in church. I slowly got away from church and started to hang out with the wrong crowd. Eventually, I got out of church altogether.

I was so far away from God and didn't want to talk about the church at all. If someone invited me to church, I would walk away, and if I had dealings with them, I wouldn't have dealings with them after that. Anyone I was close to in church I wasn't close to after I got out. I completely changed my life for the worst. Instead of learning my identity in Christ, I lived a life that wasn't me. I lived a shell of a life and was almost a robot for the devil, now that I look back.

I ran from God as fast as I could and dated several different girls. I tried to fill that void I had in my heart with females, but it didn't work. It only made the void worse. I wasn't a horrible person by the world's standards don't get me wrong. I didn't do anything worse than the other person out there. I grew up in church, so I knew in my heart it was wrong. I had enough of God to know I was wrong, and I was miserable doing it.

Being miserable didn't stop me, though, I keep trying to keep covering up being that way. Trying to put on a mask to make it look like I was happy and a man that didn't care. I didn't do an excellent job of acting like I didn't care though because I helped people out that needed help the most. I can't tell you how many times I paid someone's rent, electric, etc. for them. Maybe I was doing that to make it seem like I was godly but wasn't. To have a form of Godliness.

2 Timothy 3:5-7King James Version (KJV)

5 Having a form of godliness, but denying the power thereof: from such turn away.

6 For of this sort are they which creep into houses, and lead captive silly women laden with sins, led away with divers lusts,

7 Ever learning, and never able to come to the knowledge of the truth.

I kept living like that for a long time. Too long to count, to be honest. I do know God still helped me out. I still had money to pay my bills and had good health. I was in situations that could have killed me and should have, but I lived through it. All the time I was running from God, I ended up running into Him. God was slowly pulling me back to Him. Slowly but surely, I would find my first love once again.

A good friend of mine died of an overdose, and that hurt me. I had to miss several days of work and even get driven home from work because I had a nervous breakdown. It was a tough time to deal with. My nerves were gone completely. I had no will even to move and couldn't. I was in good health, but my emotions were shot. My parents were there for me significantly and I wouldn't have made it through that without them. The doctor put me on medication, but that didn't help a lot. It would make me in a daze, but my hands would still shake constantly.

It was a horrible time, but God started pulling me closer to Him at that time. I was under the barrel, and I had nowhere else to go but up. Someone invited me to church, so I went. I kept going back and back. God started to set me free slowly, and shortly after I got back into church, the calling of God was renewed on my life.

This might sound strange to some, but God used all those years away from Him as a teaching tool. Before I got out of church I was highly critical of ones that didn't go to church. I would look down at them in a way, and with that attitude, I wouldn't be able to reach anyone. I couldn't see them at their level at all.

One thing that changed was when I got back into church; I had a hunger to see the hurting healed. I no longer looked down at ones that weren't Christian, but I saw them as God saw them. I no longer judged them, but I saw the situations that got them into the place they were in in the first place. My outlook completely changed for the better. God used those times to overhaul my core values, that is for another book.

So, the verse

Romans 8:28King James Version (KJV)

28 And we know that all things work together for good to them that love God, to them who are the called according to his purpose.

Was very accurate for me, so I know it will be valid for you also.

Shortly after my return to the Lord, God gave me this revelation. I am writing to you in this book. That revelation freed me from the depression that followed me my whole life, and it never came back. I have never looked back on God, and now I am always looking forward. The revelation in this book is one of the reasons God put it on my heart to start Revival is Here

Church. To reach the world and see people get their true identity. I often preach that message and always will.

Shortly after returning to church, someone tried to tell me that I couldn't get back with the Lord. They said after you walk away, you can't come back. I quickly pushed that away because I know what the bible says. I have read the bible through and through, and I have never seen a verse to support that so if you have gotten away from God, don't let that stop you from coming back home.

The story of the prophet Hosea says otherwise too.

Hosea 1:2King James Version (KJV)

2 The beginning of the word of the Lord by Hosea. And the Lord said to Hosea, Go, take unto thee a wife of whoredoms and children of whoredoms: for the land hath committed great whoredom, departing from the Lord.

Hosea 3King James Version (KJV)

3 Then said the Lord unto me, Go yet, love a woman beloved of her friend, yet an adulteress, according to the love of the Lord toward the children of Israel, who look to other gods, and love flagons of wine.

2 So I bought her to me for fifteen pieces of silver, and for an homer of barley, and an half homer of barley:

3 And I said unto her, Thou shalt abide for me many days; thou shalt not play the harlot, and thou shalt not be for another man: so will I also be for thee.

4 For the children of Israel shall abide many days without a king, and without a prince, and without a sacrifice, and without an image, and without an ephod, and without teraphim:

5 Afterward shall the children of Israel return, and seek the Lord their God, and David their king; and shall fear the Lord and his goodness in the latter days.

Those are powerful verses and will change your life. Also, another excellent set of verses on the subject is the story about the prodigal son.

Luke 15:11-32 King James Version (KJV)

11 And he said, A certain man had two sons:

12 And the younger of them said to his father, Father, give me the portion of goods that falleth to me. And he divided unto them his living.

13 And not many days after the younger son gathered all together, and took his journey into a far country, and there wasted his substance with riotous living.

14 And when he had spent all, there arose a mighty famine in that land; and he began to be in want.

15 And he went and joined himself to a citizen of that country; and he sent him into his fields to feed swine.

16 And he would fain have filled his belly with the husks that the swine did eat: and no man gave unto him.

17 And when he came to himself, he said, How many hired servants of my father's have bread enough and to spare, and I perish with hunger!

18 I will arise and go to my father, and will say unto him, Father, I have sinned against heaven, and before thee,

19 And am no more worthy to be called thy son: make me as one of thy hired servants.

20 And he arose, and came to his father. But when he was yet a great way off, his father saw him, and had compassion, and ran, and fell on his neck, and kissed him.

21 And the son said unto him, Father, I have sinned against heaven, and in thy sight, and am no more worthy to be called thy son.

22 But the father said to his servants, Bring forth the best robe, and put it on him; and put a ring on his hand, and shoes on his feet:

23 And bring hither the fatted calf, and kill it; and let us eat, and be merry:

24 For this my son was dead, and is alive again; he was lost, and is found. And they began to be merry.

25 Now his elder son was in the field: and as he came and drew nigh to the house, he heard musick and dancing.

26 And he called one of the servants, and asked what these things meant.

27 And he said unto him, Thy brother is come; and thy father hath killed the fatted calf, because he hath received him safe and sound.

28 And he was angry, and would not go in: therefore came his father out, and intreated him.

29 And he answering said to his father, Lo, these many years do I serve thee, neither transgressed I at any time thy commandment: and yet thou never gavest me a kid, that I might make merry with my friends:

30 But as soon as this thy son was come, which hath devoured thy living with harlots, thou hast killed for him the fatted calf.

31 And he said unto him, Son, thou art ever with me, and all that I have is thine.

32 It was meet that we should make merry, and be glad: for this thy brother was dead, and is alive again; and was lost, and is found.

That story should be called The Story of the Loving Father.

That is a very condensed short story of my journey in Identity. Now to the teaching God gave on the subject.

Chapter 3
Laws

Joshua 1:8King James Version (KJV)

8 This book of the law shall not depart out of thy mouth; but thou shalt meditate therein day and night, that thou mayest observe to do according to all that is written therein: for then thou shalt make thy way prosperous, and then thou shalt have good success.

In order to learn about identity, it's essential to learn about Laws. In the download that God gave me about Identity, the first and foremost thing was about the laws. There are two sets of laws according to what I feel God said to me. Natural and Spiritual laws.

Spiritual Laws were given to Moses, at least the first of them, on Mt. Sinai, and he kept getting them up until his death. Exodus 20 is where the ten commandments were given. Here is a list of them but I encourage you to read it for yourself.

1. I am the Lord your God; you shall have no other gods before me.
2. You shall not use the Lord's name in vain.
3. Remember to keep the Sabbath day holy.
4. Honor your Mother and Father.
5. You shall not kill.
6. You shall not commit adultery.
7. You shall not steal.
8. You shall not bear false witness of your neighbor.
9. You shall not covet your neighbor's wife.
10. You shall not covet your neighbor's goods.

Those are just the start of the Spiritual Laws given to man. There is one about going to the bathroom.

Deuteronomy 23:12-14King James Version (KJV)
¹² Thou shalt have a place also without the camp, whither thou shalt go forth abroad:
¹³ And thou shalt have a paddle upon thy weapon; and it shall be, when thou wilt ease thyself abroad, thou shalt dig therewith, and shalt turn back and cover that which cometh from thee:
¹⁴ For the LORD thy God walketh in the midst of thy camp, to deliver thee, and to give up thine enemies

before thee; therefore shall thy camp be holy: that he see no unclean thing in thee, and turn away from thee.

The spiritual laws go into profound things on how to live, work, etc. Don't get scared now; keep reading the book. When someone says, they need to keep the law, then they need to keep the whole spiritual laws not just pick and choose.

Galatians 3:10King James Version (KJV)
¹⁰ For as many as are of the works of the law are under the curse: for it is written, Cursed is every one that continueth not in all things which are written in the book of the law to do them.

Galatians 5:3 King James Version (KJV)
³ For I testify again to every man that is circumcised, that he is a debtor to do the whole law.

So, as you can see in the previous verses if you obey the law, you have to follow it all. There is a teaching that is starting to go around the church today that for someone to make it to heaven, they must obey the ten commandments and some laws. Well, as you can see by the previous verse, it doesn't say that. It says you have to obey it all if you do obey the laws. That is dangerous teaching, too because who chooses what laws you must abide by? The person in charge, and they pick what they can obey and force others to obey it? That leads to dangerous things and will probably end up in being a cult! More on this teaching in a later chapter. I just wanted you to see what the law is.

So, as you can see, Spiritual laws are all the laws in the old testament. It tells you how you must live, eat, and other things to make it to heaven. It's a very long list of rules as you can see. Like I already said, it can get into a very tedious list of things. Not only that, but it ended up leading into men creating things and adding things to the law. Like the laws were not hard enough to keep on their own, they had to make it harder on others. That is where the law always ends up as you can see by the following verse.

Matthew 23 King James Version (KJV)

23 Then spake Jesus to the multitude, and to his disciples,

2 Saying The scribes and the Pharisees sit in Moses' seat:

3 All therefore whatsoever they bid you observe, that observe and do; but do not ye after their works: for they say, and do not.

4 For they bind heavy burdens and grievous to be borne, and lay them on men's shoulders; but they themselves will not move them with one of their fingers.

5 But all their works they do for to be seen of men: they make broad their phylacteries, and enlarge the borders of their garments,

6 And love the uppermost rooms at feasts, and the chief seats in the synagogues,

7 And greetings in the markets, and to be called of men, Rabbi, Rabbi.

8 But be not ye called Rabbi: for one is your Master, even Christ; and all ye are brethren.

9 And call no man your father upon the earth: for one is your Father, which is in heaven.

10 Neither be ye called masters: for one is your Master, even Christ.

11 But he that is greatest among you shall be your servant.

12 And whosoever shall exalt himself shall be abased; and he that shall humble himself shall be exalted.

13 But woe unto you, scribes and Pharisees, hypocrites! for ye shut up the kingdom of heaven against men: for ye neither go in yourselves, neither suffer ye them that are entering to go in.

14 Woe unto you, scribes and Pharisees, hypocrites! for ye devour widows' houses, and for a pretence make long prayer: therefore ye shall receive the greater damnation.

15 Woe unto you, scribes and Pharisees, hypocrites! for ye compass sea and land to make one proselyte, and when he is made, ye make him twofold more the child of hell than yourselves.

16 Woe unto you, ye blind guides, which say, Whosoever shall swear by the temple, it is nothing; but whosoever shall swear by the gold of the temple, he is a debtor!

17 Ye fools and blind: for whether is greater, the gold, or the temple that sanctifieth the gold?

18 And, Whosoever shall swear by the altar, it is nothing; but whosoever sweareth by the gift that is upon it, he is guilty.

19 Ye fools and blind: for whether is greater, the gift, or the altar that sanctifieth the gift?

20 Whoso therefore shall swear by the altar, sweareth by it, and by all things thereon.

21 And whoso shall swear by the temple, sweareth by it, and by him that dwelleth therein.

22 And he that shall swear by heaven, sweareth by the throne of God, and by him that sitteth thereon.

23 Woe unto you, scribes and Pharisees, hypocrites! for ye pay tithe of mint and anise and cummin, and have omitted the weightier matters of the law, judgment, mercy, and faith: these ought ye to have done, and not to leave the other undone.

Chan Smith

24 Ye blind guides, which strain at a gnat, and swallow a camel.

25 Woe unto you, scribes and Pharisees, hypocrites! for ye make clean the outside of the cup and of the platter, but within they are full of extortion and excess.

26 Thou blind Pharisee, cleanse first that which is within the cup and platter, that the outside of them may be clean also.

27 Woe unto you, scribes and Pharisees, hypocrites! for ye are like unto whited sepulchres, which indeed appear beautiful outward, but are within full of dead men's bones, and of all uncleanness.

28 Even so ye also outwardly appear righteous unto men, but within ye are full of hypocrisy and iniquity.

29 Woe unto you, scribes and Pharisees, hypocrites! because ye build the tombs of the prophets, and garnish the sepulchres of the righteous,

84

30 And say, If we had been in the days of our fathers, we would not have been partakers with them in the blood of the prophets.

31 Wherefore ye be witnesses unto yourselves, that ye are the children of them which killed the prophets.

32 Fill ye up then the measure of your fathers.

33 Ye serpents, ye generation of vipers, how can ye escape the damnation of hell?

34 Wherefore, behold, I send unto you prophets, and wise men, and scribes: and some of them ye shall kill and crucify; and some of them shall ye scourge in your synagogues, and persecute them from city to city:

35 That upon you may come all the righteous blood shed upon the earth, from the blood of righteous Abel unto the blood of Zacharias son of Barachias, whom ye slew between the temple and the altar.

36 Verily I say unto you, All these things shall come upon this generation.

37 O Jerusalem, Jerusalem, thou that killest the prophets, and stonest them which are sent unto thee, how often would I have gathered thy children together, even as a hen gathereth her chickens under her wings, and ye would not!

38 Behold, your house is left unto you desolate.

39 For I say unto you, Ye shall not see me henceforth, till ye shall say, Blessed is he that cometh in the name of the Lord.

So, as you can see; men ended up making laws to suit their own needs, and it ended up in control.

Now, we will talk about where the spiritual laws came from, how they came into being, and why. This is important because we need to get a full understanding of the law before we can talk about identity. Bear with me on this as we continue on this learning journey together.

Israel chose to have laws and not a relationship with God. They got afraid for whatever reason and decided to have one man hear from God and tell them what God said, like a mediator of sorts. They chose to have a person talk to them instead of God directly. They even went so far as to say they could obey the laws. That was a very prideful statement to make and a very costly one at that. You can read about that happening in Exodus 19 and the following verse.

Exodus 20:18-21King James Version (KJV)

18 And all the people saw the thunderings, and the lightnings, and the noise of the trumpet, and the mountain smoking: and when the people saw it, they removed, and stood afar off.

19 And they said unto Moses, Speak thou with us, and we will hear: but let not God speak with us, lest we die.

20 And Moses said unto the people, Fear not: for God is come to prove you, and that his fear may be before your faces, that ye sin not.

21 And the people stood afar off, and Moses drew near unto the thick darkness where God was.

By reading Exodus 19 and Exodus 29:18-21, you can see the people chose the law and were afraid of God. They said they could do it. Something very interesting happened after they said that. More laws were given as you can see in the following verses.

Exodus 20:22-26King James Version (KJV)

22 And the Lord said unto Moses, Thus thou shalt say unto the children of Israel, Ye have seen that I have talked with you from heaven.

23 Ye shall not make with me gods of silver, neither shall ye make unto you gods of gold.

24 An altar of earth thou shalt make unto me, and shalt sacrifice thereon thy burnt offerings, and thy peace offerings, thy sheep, and thine oxen: in all places where I record my name I will come unto thee, and I will bless thee.

25 And if thou wilt make me an altar of stone, thou shalt not build it of hewn stone: for if thou lift up thy tool upon it, thou hast polluted it.

26 Neither shalt thou go up by steps unto mine altar, that thy nakedness be not discovered thereon.

Natural laws are laws of nature like, if you walk on water you sink. If you light something on fire, it burns. ETC. Everyone who has taken any schooling at all knows about these laws, so I don't need to get into detail about them.

Another example of natural law is if you are around someone with the flu and you're not immune to it chances are you will get the flu. Another one is if your family has a history of cancer, you have a high chance to get cancer. I am adding these examples for a reason. Keep reading this book, and I will explain why.

Laws are a very real part of life. On your own, you can't escape the laws or the penalties of them, both spiritual and natural laws. Some of you reading this book have heard of the spiritual laws, but you haven't thought about the naturals laws, but they will and do affect your life every second of the day. Regardless if you believe in them or not, the same goes with spiritual laws. Even if you don't want to be under them or believe in them both, you are. On your own, that is. I will explain that statement in a later chapter.

Chapter 4
Jesus

Matthew 2:1–12 King James Version (KJV)

2 Now when Jesus was born in Bethlehem of Judaea in the days of Herod the king, behold, there came wise men from the east to Jerusalem,

Next, lets us look at the life of Jesus. He is fundamental to this book on Identity and everyone on the earth. Not looking at His life would mean a false book on Identity. I want to look at His life before I go any further in this download I got from God, so everyone is on the same page. You might ask why He is so important? Keep reading the book you will find out.

Jesus had a very miraculous birth. Some already know this story, but let's still go over this to refresh everyone's memory, ok? In Luke 1 and 2, we have an account of that birth.

In those verses, Jesus was born a virgin birth. An angel appeared to Mary, the mother of Jesus, to tell her what was about to happen, and she said it was ok with her. (I am putting this in my language so everyone will understand. It's hard to understand King James Version of the Bible.) She was engaged to be married to Joseph, a carpenter by trade, and in those days, that was a no-no for a female to be pregnant out of marriage. Joseph found out she was pregnant and he was going to call off the wedding but do it in a way that it didn't shame Mary. He was being nice to her as much as possible because he felt at; first, she had cheated on him. He found out what happened when an angel appeared to him and told him. He agreed to marry her and to be the fathers Step-Dad. That brings us up to the birth of Jesus.

When Mary was about ready to give birth, a law came down from the government that everyone had to go to their home town for the census. Mary and Joseph had to go to Bethlehem because they both were from the house of David.

When they got to their destination, they couldn't find any rooms in the Inns. Because of the law, everyone was in town filling up everyplace they could. Joseph, worried about his wife, her about to give birth made him worry more, looked everywhere. He found a stable and being that was the only place he could find, took it. He didn't know that was all prophesied about Jesus's birth.

Mary gave birth, and they named him Jesus because of the angel's personal prophesy. The only place they could put Jesus was a manger. That, too, was prophesied long ago. They had visitors at the stable to glorify God and to see the newborn child, a savior.

Later, when they were at their home, wise men came and brought them gifts. The presents helped much because Mary and Joseph were warned to go to Egypt to save Jesus's life. The wise men came a long way, from the area of what is now Iraq, to see Jesus. They were guided by a supernatural star all the way.

They stopped to see King Herod, and he received them. Herod tried to smooth talk them to get information about where Jesus was because Herod was jealous. God warned them in a dream, though, and that dream prevented them from giving the location up. Praise God for dreams and visions. In Matthew 2:1-12, it talks about the wise men. I encourage you to read that in your bible.

The following verse is about Joseph and Mary being warned to leave for Egypt. The gifts the wise men brought greatly helped with that escape. God provides.

Matthew 2:3-13King James Version (KJV)

3 When Herod the king had heard these things, he was troubled, and all Jerusalem with him.

4 And when he had gathered all the chief priests and scribes of the people together, he demanded of them where Christ should be born.

5 And they said unto him, In Bethlehem of Judaea: for thus it is written by the prophet,

6 And thou Bethlehem, in the land of Juda, art not the least among the princes of Juda: for out of thee shall come a Governor, that shall rule my people Israel.

7 Then Herod, when he had privily called the wise men, enquired of them diligently what time the star appeared.

8 And he sent them to Bethlehem, and said, Go and search diligently for the young child; and when ye have found him, bring me word again, that I may come and worship him also.

9 When they had heard the king, they departed; and, lo, the star, which they saw in the east, went before them, till it came and stood over where the young child was.

10 When they saw the star, they rejoiced with exceeding great joy.

11 And when they were come into the house, they saw the young child with Mary his mother, and fell down, and worshipped him: and when they had opened their treasures, they presented unto him gifts; gold, and frankincense and myrrh.

12 And being warned of God in a dream that they should not return to Herod, they departed into their own country another way.

13 And when they were departed, behold, the angel of the Lord appeareth to Joseph in a dream, saying, Arise, and take the young child and his mother, and flee into Egypt, and be thou there until I bring thee word: for Herod will seek the young child to destroy him.

As you can see by that passage, Mary and Joseph were warned to leave and go to Egypt, because of that warning Jesus's life was saved. Praise God for that too.

Herod was jealous of the prophecies about Jesus, but Herod misinterpreted those words.

Jesus's kingdom wasn't of this world.

John 18:36 King James Version (KJV)

36 Jesus answered, My kingdom is not of this world: if my kingdom were of this world, then would my servants fight, that I should not be delivered to the Jews: but now is my kingdom not from hence.

While Joseph, Mary, and Jesus were in Egypt, Herod killed a massive number of children because of his jealousy. He was afraid of losing his crown. That story is in the following verses.

Matthew 2:13-23King James Version (KJV)

13 And when they were departed, behold, the angel of the Lord appeareth to Joseph in a dream, saying, Arise, and take the young child and his mother, and flee into Egypt, and be thou there until I bring thee word: for Herod will seek the young child to destroy him.

14 When he arose, he took the young child and his mother by night, and departed into Egypt:

15 And was there until the death of Herod: that it might be fulfilled which was spoken of the Lord by the prophet, saying, Out of Egypt have I called my son.

16 Then Herod, when he saw that he was mocked of the wise men, was exceeding wroth, and sent forth, and slew all the children that were in Bethlehem, and in all the coasts thereof, from two years old and under, according to the time which he had diligently inquired of the wise men.

17 Then was fulfilled that which was spoken by Jeremiah the prophet, saying,

18 In Rama was there a voice heard, lamentation, and weeping, and great mourning, Rachel weeping for her children, and would not be comforted, because they are not.

19 But when Herod was dead, behold, an angel of the Lord appeareth in a dream to Joseph in Egypt,

20 Saying, Arise, and take the young child and his mother, and go into the land of Israel: for they are dead which sought the young child's life.

21 And he arose, and took the young child and his mother, and came into the land of Israel.

22 But when he heard that Archelaus did reign in Judaea in the room of his father Herod, he was afraid to go thither: notwithstanding, being warned of God in a dream, he turned aside into the parts of Galilee:

23 And he came and dwelt in a city called Nazareth: that it might be fulfilled which was spoken by the prophets, He shall be called a Nazarene.

As you can see, that was a very tragic time, and much weeping was done. That action set the course for Herod's reign and his descendants.

At an early age, Jesus was thinking about His father in Heaven. He was mindful of what God the Father wanted, and He did it. One day His mother was traveling and couldn't find Jesus anywhere. So, she went back to find him in Jerusalem and found Him at the temple. That story is in the following verses.

Luke 2:41-52 King James Version (KJV)

41 Now his parents went to Jerusalem every year at the feast of the passover.

42 And when he was twelve years old, they went up to Jerusalem after the custom of the feast.

43 And when they had fulfilled the days, as they returned, the child Jesus tarried behind in Jerusalem; and Joseph and his mother knew not of it.

44 But they, supposing him to have been in the company, went a day's journey; and they sought him among their kinsfolk and acquaintance.

45 And when they found him not, they turned back again to Jerusalem, seeking him.

46 And it came to pass, that after three days they found him in the temple, sitting in the midst of the doctors, both hearing them, and asking them questions.

47 And all that heard him were astonished at his understanding and answers.

48 And when they saw him, they were amazed: and his mother said unto him, Son, why hast thou thus dealt with us? behold, thy father and I have sought thee sorrowing.

49 And he said unto them, How is it that ye sought me? wist ye not that I must be about my Father's business?

50 And they understood not the saying which he spake unto them.

51 And he went down with them, and came to Nazareth, and was subject unto them: but his mother kept all these sayings in her heart.

52 And Jesus increased in wisdom and stature, and in favour with God and man.

Jesus went around doing miracles everywhere he went.

Matthew 12:15King James Version (KJV)
15 But when Jesus knew it, he withdrew himself from thence: and great multitudes followed him, and he healed them all;

His first miracle happened at a wedding He attended. They were all celebrating and ran out of wine. Jesus told them to fill the water pots to the brim, meaning up to the very top. I thought it was something that He didn't even pray over it; He just told them to fill it up and then to draw some out then give it to the governor of the feast, the one in charge.

That was a risky thing to do, but they obeyed Him faithfully. Mary told them to do whatever Jesus said, so that could have been one of the reasons. Whatever reasons they did, I am sure they were thrilled they did obey. Everyone loved the wine and said it was the best wine of the feast. I would go as far as to say it was probably the best wine they ever had because God always does everything to its best, right? He made you.

I will share with you the verses for this story then share some more thoughts on it.

John 2:1-11King James Version (KJV)

2 And the third day there was a marriage in Cana of Galilee; and the mother of Jesus was there:

2 And both Jesus was called, and his disciples, to the marriage.

3 And when they wanted wine, the mother of Jesus saith unto him, They have no wine.

4 Jesus saith unto her, Woman, what have I to do with thee? mine hour is not yet come.

5 His mother saith unto the servants, Whatsoever he saith unto you, do it.

6 And there were set there six waterpots of stone, after the manner of the purifying of the Jews, containing two or three firkins apiece.

7 Jesus saith unto them, Fill the waterpots with water. And they filled them up to the brim.

8 And he saith unto them, Draw out now, and bear unto the governor of the feast. And they bare it.

9 When the ruler of the feast had tasted the water that was made wine, and knew not whence it was: (but the servants which drew the water knew;) the governor of the feast called the bridegroom,

10 And saith unto him, Every man at the beginning doth set forth good wine; and when men have well drunk, then that which is worse: but thou hast kept the good wine until now.

11 This beginning of miracles did Jesus in Cana of Galilee, and manifested forth his glory; and his disciples believed on him.

There are several points I would like to point out and talk about in that story. First of all, as I already said, Mary, the mother of Jesus, pushed Jesus into doing the miracle. His reply at first was, "It wasn't my time." His mother didn't take no for an answer and just turned around to the workers and said: "do whatever He says to do." Very interesting indeed, and I could write a whole chapter on that.

Going by personal experience, sometimes we need a push to get into the ministry. It's hard to take that first step and someone having faith in you and not taking no for an answer is what we need. I am not saying that was the case for Jesus. Maybe He did it that way to teach us. That it's ok to have a push to get into the ministry and perhaps even preferred. I don't believe in anyone just deciding to start a ministry without anyone's blessing and ok. That is for another book, though. I do feel though that we can get that lesson out of that story.

A mom knows best on when we are ready for ministry as does she on a lot of things. Even today, I still look toward my parents for guidance and thoughts on things. I always will no matter how old I am. That is one thing God created the family unit for, to lean on each other for support and guidance. Who better knows you, besides God, of course, than the people who raised you and known you since well your birth?

Another point is, the very first thing He did. His first miracle was making wine. It was new wine then correct? That makes me think of the new wine of the Holy Spirit. I also feel it was saying, **"God is doing a new thing on the earth."**

Jesus did several other miracles in His life on earth. There are too many to mention here, though.

John 21:25 King James Version (KJV)

25 And there are also many other things which Jesus did, the which, if they should be written every one, I suppose that even the world itself could not contain the books that should be written. Amen.

All miracles are great no matter how small we might think so I don't want anyone to take me wrong here, but one of the biggest miracles is when Jesus raised Lazarus from the dead.

Lazarus was dead for four days and already in his tomb. He and his sisters were friends with Jesus. When Jesus got there, several people were crying and mourning. Jesus told them to roll the stone away.

I know today it's hard to place what rolling a stone away means. Today, we have graves dug into the ground for burial, but in those days, it was common to have caves cut into the rock for graves. They had a large round stone cut for a door to the cave. The stone was flat on both sides and could be rolled right to the left. There was a little ditch on one end of the stone as a guide path for the stone to roll in; otherwise, it would fall over.

When they rolled the stone away, Jesus said the following words, "Lazarus come forth." Lazarus came walking out of the grave, and I am sure a few were surprised to see him. You see, they told Jesus he smelled already because he had been in there a few days. That didn't stop Jesus because He had faith Lazarus would be alive again.

I am sure Lazarus was walking very strangely coming out of the grave. You might ask why? Well, he was wrapped up in grave clothes still. Jesus told them to remove the grave clothes from him. That was a powerful story, and I love sharing it. That can be found in John 11; I encourage you to read that to get the full story.

Jesus was eventually put on an illegal trial by the religious leaders of the time. They went and found people to testify against Him falsely, and then they illegally found Him guilty. They took Him to the Roman leader of the time over the area, Pontius Pilate, to have Jesus put to death.

At first, Pontius Pilate wasn't going to yield to their demands, but finally, he did. Jesus was sentenced to death on the cross. You can find the account in Luke 22 and 23 in your bible.

Let's talk about who Jesus is; Jesus is the son of God and became flesh and lived a sinless life. He died on the Cross so we can get into heaven. Without Him, we wouldn't be able to get into heaven. I will talk more about that in another Chapter.

Jesus life is a very important part of Identity. When I got the download of this book, I was never the same again. It changed me forever.

As you read in the chapter when I wrote briefly about my life, I had depression problems and lousy self-esteem issues. For me to write this book about identity is proof enough how it changed my life. I know your life will change too.

Chapter 5
Who was/is Jesus?

Matthew 1:18King James Version (KJV)

18 Now the birth of Jesus Christ was on this wise: When as his mother Mary was espoused to Joseph, before they came together, she was found with child of the Holy Ghost.

*I*n the previous chapter, I write on the life of Jesus, about His birth, what He did, and how He died. Now I will talk about who He was and is. I first wanted to share what Jesus did first before going into who He is. Most of the information was shared in the previous chapter, so this chapter will not be as long.

I pray I still have your attention, and you're still reading. I know sometimes it's hard to keep the focus on a book because I have that problem too. I can only really get into a book if the anointing is on it, so I pray it's on this one also.

Now let's go into who Jesus was and is. We will also go into why He had to live that life and die the way He did.

Like I said in the previous chapter, Jesus was born of a virgin birth. You might ask what that means? Well, that means that His mother didn't sleep with a man to conceive, The Holy Spirit conceived him. You can find that in the following verse.

Matthew 1:18King James Version (KJV)

18 Now the birth of Jesus Christ was on this wise: When as his mother Mary was espoused to Joseph, before they came together, she was found with child of the Holy Ghost.

Jesus had to be born that way because He came to free us from sin and be the Passover lamb for us all. As you read in a previous chapter on the law, it was impossible to keep the law on our own. It also says in another verse, we have all sinned.

Romans 3:23King James Version (KJV)

23 For all have sinned, and come short of the glory of God;

The bible verse about Jesus being the Passover lamb is the following.

1 Corinthians 5:7King James Version (KJV)

7 Purge out therefore the old leaven, that ye may be a new lump, as ye are unleavened. For even Christ our passover is sacrificed for us:

Now that we talked about Jesus being the Passover lamb and how He was conceived, let's talk about who He was and is. Jesus was and is God that came in the flesh. He was the son of God too. I know that can be a lot to take in. Was He God or the son of God? The answer to that is both. I am not going to get into doctrine here and make anyone mad. That isn't the point of this book. The main thing you need to know and believe though is He was and is both God and the son of God. I will share with you some verses so you can read them.

John 1King James Version (KJV)

1 In the beginning was the Word, and the Word was with God, and the Word was God.

2 The same was in the beginning with God.

3 All things were made by him; and without him was not any thing made that was made.

4 In him was life; and the life was the light of men.

5 And the light shineth in darkness; and the darkness comprehended it not.

6 There was a man sent from God, whose name was John.

7 The same came for a witness, to bear witness of the Light, that all men through him might believe.

8 He was not that Light, but was sent to bear witness of that Light.

9 That was the true Light, which lighteth every man that cometh into the world.

10 He was in the world, and the world was made by him, and the world knew him not.

11 He came unto his own, and his own received him not.

12 But as many as received him, to them gave he power to become the sons of God, even to them that believe on his name:

13 Which were born, not of blood, nor of the will of the flesh, nor of the will of man, but of God.

14 And the Word was made flesh, and dwelt among us, (and we beheld his glory, the glory as of the only begotten of the Father,) full of grace and truth.

15 John bare witness of him, and cried, saying, This was he of whom I spake, He that cometh after me is preferred before me: for he was before me.

16 And of his fulness have all we received, and grace for grace.

17 For the law was given by Moses, but grace and truth came by Jesus Christ.

18 No man hath seen God at any time, the only begotten Son, which is in the bosom of the Father, he hath declared him.

John 10:30King James Version (KJV)

30 I and my Father are one.

John 5:19-29King James Version (KJV)

19 Then answered Jesus and said unto them, Verily, verily, I say unto you, The Son can do nothing of himself, but what he seeth the Father do: for what things soever he doeth, these also doeth the Son likewise.

20 For the Father loveth the Son, and sheweth him all things that himself doeth: and he will shew him greater works than these, that ye may marvel.

21 For as the Father raiseth up the dead, and quickeneth them; even so the Son quickeneth whom he will.

22 For the Father judgeth no man, but hath committed all judgment unto the Son:

23 That all men should honour the Son, even as they honour the Father. He that honoureth not the Son honoureth not the Father which hath sent him.

24 Verily, verily, I say unto you, He that heareth my word, and believeth on him that sent me, hath everlasting life, and shall not come into condemnation; but is passed from death unto life.

25 Verily, verily, I say unto you, The hour is coming, and now is, when the dead shall hear the voice of the Son of God: and they that hear shall live.

26 For as the Father hath life in himself; so hath he given to the Son to have life in himself;

27 And hath given him authority to execute judgment also, because he is the Son of man.

28 Marvel not at this: for the hour is coming, in the which all that are in the graves shall hear his voice,

29 And shall come forth; they that have done good, unto the resurrection of life; and they that have done evil, unto the resurrection of damnation.

Those are some powerful verses to remember as a Christian and especially for witnessing. I know most of you know the things in this chapter and the previous. For you, this isn't a revelation at all, but I want to tell you that this book will be read by many. Some don't know that so it's essential for everyone to be on the same page.

I tend to take for granted about the simplest things of the Bible, but the simplest things are the ones that need to be preached. We tend to make the bible and the gospel of the kingdom very hard, but it isn't at all. It's easy, and that is the purity and good of it. So, reading this over can reset us. Let us see what it's really about. In the next few chapters, I will share more how this ties into identity, and you will know the gospel is what identity is all about.

I could share with you many more bible verses on who Jesus was and is but I think you get the picture. As I said, the verses are powerful, and I encourage you to read them often.

Now let's talk about Jesus living a sinless life. I will share with you some verses then explain them to you. If you are a highlighter, then I encourage you to highlight the verses I am about to share with you.

1 Peter 2:22King James Version (KJV)

22 Who did no sin, neither was guile found in his mouth:

2 Corinthians 5:21King James Version (KJV)

21 For he hath made him to be sin for us, who knew no sin; that we might be made the righteousness of God in him.

Hebrews 4:15King James Version (KJV)

15 For we have not an high priest which cannot be touched with the feeling of our infirmities; but was in all points tempted like as we are, yet without sin.

1 John 3:5King James Version (KJV)

5 And ye know that he was manifested to take away our sins; and in him is no sin.

As you can see, there was no sin in Him at all. I want to explain that to you more so you can understand more about it. I know some of you already know that but might not have a good understanding. Jesus's blood came from His father. So, there was no sin in Him because of that fact. That is a powerful thing to think about. So, there was literally no sin in Him.

Next thing I want to talk about is that Jesus is our savior. As you read in the chapter about the law, it's impossible to live our whole life from birth to death without sin. Only one did that, and He was Jesus. His sinless life, death on the cross, and raised from the dead is the only way we can be forgiven of sin.

1 John 4:20King James Version (KJV)

20 If a man say, I love God, and hateth his brother, he is a liar: for he that loveth not his brother whom he hath seen, how can he love God whom he hath not seen?

Luke 2:11King James Version (KJV)

11 For unto you is born this day in the city of David a Saviour, which is Christ the Lord.

Let's talk about Jesus dying on the cross for us. Jesus had to die on the cross in place of us for our sins. I talked about in the previous chapter how Jesus died on the cross now let's talk about what happened afterward.

As you read in the previous chapter, they came to anoint Jesus body with spices, but I didn't go into what happened when they got there. Mary saw two angels, and they said to them, "He isn't here, He has risen." That is paraphrasing. You can read the full account in the following verses of the bible.

Luke 24King James Version (KJV)

24 Now upon the first day of the week, very early in the morning, they came unto the sepulchre, bringing the spices which they had prepared, and certain others with them.

2 And they found the stone rolled away from the sepulchre.

3 And they entered in, and found not the body of the Lord Jesus.

4 And it came to pass, as they were much perplexed thereabout, behold, two men stood by them in shining garments:

5 And as they were afraid, and bowed down their faces to the earth, they said unto them, Why seek ye the living among the dead?

6 He is not here, but is risen: remember how he spake unto you when he was yet in Galilee,

7 Saying, The Son of man must be delivered into the hands of sinful men, and be crucified, and the third day rise again.

8 And they remembered his words,

9 And returned from the sepulchre, and told all these things unto the eleven, and to all the rest.

10 It was Mary Magdalene and Joanna, and Mary the mother of James, and other women that were with them, which told these things unto the apostles.

11 And their words seemed to them as idle tales, and they believed them not.

12 Then arose Peter, and ran unto the sepulchre; and stooping down, he beheld the linen clothes laid by themselves, and departed, wondering in himself at that which was come to pass.

13 And, behold, two of them went that same day to a village called Emmaus, which was from Jerusalem about threescore furlongs.

14 And they talked together of all these things which had happened.

15 And it came to pass, that, while they communed together and reasoned, Jesus himself drew near, and went with them.

16 But their eyes were holden that they should not know him.

17 And he said unto them, What manner of communications are these that ye have one to another, as ye walk, and are sad?

18 And the one of them, whose name was Cleopas, answering said unto him, Art thou only a stranger in Jerusalem, and hast not known the things which are come to pass there in these days?

19 And he said unto them, What things? And they said unto him, Concerning Jesus of Nazareth, which was a prophet mighty in deed and word before God and all the people:

20 And how the chief priests and our rulers delivered him to be condemned to death, and have crucified him.

21 But we trusted that it had been he which should have redeemed Israel: and beside all this, to day is the third day since these things were done.

22 Yea, and certain women also of our company made us astonished, which were early at the sepulchre;

23 And when they found not his body, they came, saying, that they had also seen a vision of angels, which said that he was alive.

24 And certain of them which were with us went to the sepulchre, and found it even so as the women had said: but him they saw not.

25 Then he said unto them, O fools, and slow of heart to believe all that the prophets have spoken:

26 Ought not Christ to have suffered these things, and to enter into his glory?

27 And beginning at Moses and all the prophets, he expounded unto them in all the scriptures the things concerning himself.

28 And they drew nigh unto the village, whither they went: and he made as though he would have gone further.

29 But they constrained him, saying, Abide with us: for it is toward evening, and the day is far spent. And he went in to tarry with them.

30 And it came to pass, as he sat at meat with them, he took bread, and blessed it, and brake, and gave to them.

31 And their eyes were opened, and they knew him; and he vanished out of their sight.

32 And they said one to another, Did not our heart burn within us, while he talked with us by the way, and while he opened to us the scriptures?

33 And they rose up the same hour, and returned to Jerusalem, and found the eleven gathered together, and them that were with them,

34 Saying, The Lord is risen indeed, and hath appeared to Simon.

35 And they told what things were done in the way, and how he was known of them in breaking of bread.

36 And as they thus spake, Jesus himself stood in the midst of them, and saith unto them, Peace be unto you.

37 But they were terrified and affrighted, and supposed that they had seen a spirit.

38 And he said unto them, Why are ye troubled? and why do thoughts arise in your hearts?

39 Behold my hands and my feet, that it is I myself: handle me, and see; for a spirit hath not flesh and bones, as ye see me have.

40 And when he had thus spoken, he shewed them his hands and his feet.

41 And while they yet believed not for joy, and wondered, he said unto them, Have ye here any meat?

42 And they gave him a piece of a broiled fish, and of an honeycomb.

43 And he took it, and did eat before them.

44 And he said unto them, These are the words which I spake unto you, while I was yet with you, that all things must be fulfilled, which were written in the law of Moses, and in the prophets, and in the psalms, concerning me.

45 Then opened he their understanding, that they might understand the scriptures,

46 And said unto them, Thus it is written, and thus it behooved Christ to suffer, and to rise from the dead the third day:

47 And that repentance and remission of sins should be preached in his name among all nations, beginning at Jerusalem.
48 And ye are witnesses of these things.
49 And, behold, I send the promise of my Father upon you: but tarry ye in the city of Jerusalem, until ye be endued with power from on high.
50 And he led them out as far as to Bethany, and he lifted up his hands, and blessed them.
51 And it came to pass, while he blessed them, he was parted from them, and carried up into heaven.
52 And they worshipped him, and returned to Jerusalem with great joy:
53 And were continually in the temple, praising and blessing God. Amen.

There is one more main point I want to share about Jesus before we can move on to the next chapter. Jesus is the only way to heaven. I know some people don't believe that and say it was never mentioned, but I will show you in scripture that He did. That is very important to know. That is a good thing though because it's not by our own works, I will share more about that in a later chapter. The scripture of Jesus saying, "He is the only way" is the following.

John 14:6King James Version (KJV)
6 Jesus saith unto him, I am the way, the truth,
and the life: no man cometh unto the Father, but by me.

That one verse proves He said that and is one of the most important verses to know in the bible. I encourage you to memorize it; you will need it in the future if you ever try to lead anyone to the Lord.

After Jesus talked to the disciples, He ascended to heaven. They stood there looking up until an angel said, "Why are you just standing here looking up." Well, that is a paraphrase, but the point I feel they were trying to make is, "Don't just stand here looking up, go do what He told you to do. Go spread the gospel of the kingdom around the world." We are still just standing there waiting for Him to return today instead of doing the great commission. That is another book, though.

The following verses are about Him ascending into heaven and the great commission.

Acts 1:1-11King James Version (KJV)
1 The former treatise have I made, O Theophilus, of
all that Jesus began both to do and teach,
2 Until the day in which he was taken up, after that
he through the Holy Ghost had given commandments
unto the apostles whom he had chosen:

3 To whom also he shewed himself alive after his passion by many infallible proofs, being seen of them forty days, and speaking of the things pertaining to the kingdom of God:

4 And, being assembled together with them, commanded them that they should not depart from Jerusalem, but wait for the promise of the Father, which, saith he, ye have heard of me.

5 For John truly baptized with water; but ye shall be baptized with the Holy Ghost not many days hence.

6 When they therefore were come together, they asked of him, saying, Lord, wilt thou at this time restore again the kingdom to Israel?

7 And he said unto them, It is not for you to know the times or the seasons, which the Father hath put in his own power.

8 But ye shall receive power, after that the Holy Ghost is come upon you: and ye shall be witnesses unto me both in Jerusalem, and in all Judaea, and in Samaria, and unto the uttermost part of the earth.

9 And when he had spoken these things, while they beheld, he was taken up; and a cloud received him out of their sight.

10 And while they looked stedfastly toward heaven as he went up, behold, two men stood by them in white apparel;

11 Which also said, Ye men of Galilee, why stand ye gazing up into heaven? this same Jesus, which is taken up from you into heaven, shall so come in like manner as ye have seen him go into heaven.

Matthew 28:16-20King James Version (KJV)
16 Then the eleven disciples went away into Galilee, into a mountain where Jesus had appointed them.
17 And when they saw him, they worshipped him: but some doubted.
18 And Jesus came and spake unto them, saying, All power is given unto me in heaven and in earth.
19 Go ye therefore, and teach all nations, baptizing them in the name of the Father, and of the Son, and of the Holy Ghost:
20 Teaching them to observe all things whatsoever I have commanded you: and, lo, I am with you always, even unto the end of the world. Amen.

So, let's put together everything talked about in this chapter. Jesus was/is God, the Son of God, the Passover Lamb, and savior. He is also the only way into heaven. He lived a sinless life. Died on the cross and rose from the dead on the third day then ascended to heaven.

For some, that is a lot to take in, and you can only wholly receive it by faith. Don't try to understand it with your mind because it must be grasped with your spirit.

Hebrews 11:6King James Version (KJV)

6 But without faith it is impossible to please him: for he that cometh to God must believe that he is, and that he is a rewarder of them that diligently seek him.

Many have fallen into and have started cults because they tried to understand that all with their mind. Now let's go to the next chapter.

Chapter 6
New Person

Romans 12:2King James Version (KJV)

2 And be not conformed to this world: but be ye transformed by the renewing of your mind, that ye may prove what is that good, and acceptable, and perfect, will of God.

I f you didn't get scared off by the chapter of the Law, reading this chapter will let you know why I added it to this book. It was important for everyone to understand what the law was.

As you saw, no one can obey the law on their own. It's impossible to do. Even if you made up your mind one day that you were going to obey the law, and you somehow did obey it all, what about before that? What about those times that you messed up in the past? If you obeyed the law, you would have to obey it pretty much from birth to death for it to work. Even then, it's limited, and according to my studies, you probably will not make it into heaven. I am talking about even if you obeyed it all from birth to death, every little dot even. Which it's impossible to obey it all in the first place.

This verse says it best when it comes to that.

Romans 3:23King James Version (KJV)

23 For all have sinned, and come short of the glory of God;

Here are two more verse that drives that point home.

Romans 3:10-12King James Version (KJV)

10 As it is written, There is none righteous, no, not one:

11 There is none that understandeth, there is none that seeketh after God.

12 They are all gone out of the way, they are together become unprofitable; there is none that doeth good, no, not one.

Isaiah 64:6King James Version (KJV)

6 But we are all as an unclean thing, and all our righteousnesses are as filthy rags; and we all do fade as a leaf; and our iniquities, like the wind, have taken us away.

That pretty much sums us up, I mean us on our own. I am sure most of you have already heard that and are already born-again. It's good to have a refresher though and to get everyone on the same page.

Now, let's go into some teaching that you might not have heard. I have preached this many times in the past, and I am sure I will preach it many more times, but I have not or will not go over it like I will in this book. It's hard to go into in-depth teaching when preaching. Often, Holy Spirit will direct me another way because someone needs to hear something, a right now word. So, it's hard for me to go into depth with it. Also, the sermon would be very long if it was to be gone over in-depth, and I would end up having to pick someone off the floor because they fell asleep. Maybe even have to raise them from the dead as Paul did. ☺

Acts 20:9King James Version (KJV)

9 And there sat in a window a certain young man named Eutychus, being fallen into a deep sleep: and as Paul was long preaching, he sunk down with sleep, and fell down from the third loft, and was taken up dead.

Let's look at the law. The law has no power on its own. It can't give you the power to obey it; the law only says what you can't do or how to do it. It can't give you any ability or a special gift to do it. It can't protect you from it; it can't stop the drive to do something even. To put it bluntly, the law is dead. There is no relationship in the law; it's just a set of rules that you can go through your life striving to do.

Let me put it another way: living the law would be like a robot. The robot has a set of code in it that tells it what to do. It has rules, do this, do that, don't do that, etc. It can't go out of those rules. It can't do anything but what it's programmed to do. There is no relationship with it, at least at the time of writing this.

Your life would be like being a robot living the law. It would be dry and dead with no relationship with God at all. That doesn't sound like this verse at all.

John 10:10King James Version (KJV)

10 The thief cometh not, but for to steal, and to kill, and to destroy: I am come that they might have life, and that they might have it more abundantly.

My goal is for you to have an abundant life after reading this book. I pray that I give you the tools to do it to.

Now let me share with you the verse proving to you that the law has no power on its own.

Romans 8:3-4King James Version (KJV)

3 For what the law could not do, in that it was weak through the flesh, God sending his own Son in the likeness of sinful flesh, and for sin, condemned sin in the flesh:

4 That the righteousness of the law might be fulfilled in us, who walk not after the flesh, but after the Spirit.

As you can see by that verse, the law has no power on its own. It can't give you any power to do it. Grace, however, gives you the power to obey it. Graces changes you forever. It's empowerment and change. Let me give you some examples to get my point across.

Every state in America has speed limits set on how fast you can drive. In Kentucky, right now the speed limit is 70 miles per hour on the main interstates that don't go through cities. That speed limit doesn't give you the power to obey it; it merely states what the speed limit is. You have a choice to obey it or not. Not obeying it, you have to pay the consequences. How fast you drive over will affect how much you pay for it. If you drive over to speed limit, you can lose your driver's licenses. Do you see it?

The spiritual laws are like that. They tell you what you should or shouldn't do, but all they do is tell you. Without the spirit, you don't have any power to obey it. You survive only by your willpower alone.

With grace, you have the power to obey it. I often say grace is much deeper than the law. You often see people under grace living purer lives not because they are forced to or trying to but because they want to.

I like to describe it this way. When you are married to someone, over the years, the closer you become you stop doing the things they dislike. Not because you are forced to but because you want to please them. You want to make them happy, and making them happy makes you happy. Why? Because you love them! Am I making any sense? I pray I am.

I have noticed that you can always tell who has been married for a long time because they walk the same, sit the same, talk the same, and can tell what the other is thinking. The longer they are with them, they become like the other person. They aren't doing that because they are forced to be like the other, but they just become that naturally, over time. That is what happens out of love. The one you truly love affects you, whether you like it or not. It just happens. That is a powerful thing.

It reminds me of a few bible verses I like.

2 Corinthians 3:18King James Version (KJV)

18 But we all, with open face beholding as in a glass the glory of the Lord, are changed into the same image from glory to glory, even as by the Spirit of the Lord.

Romans 12:2King James Version (KJV)

2 And be not conformed to this world: but be ye transformed by the renewing of your mind, that ye may prove what is that good, and acceptable, and perfect, will of God.

Romans 12:2King James Version (KJV)

2 And be not conformed to this world: but be ye transformed by the renewing of your mind, that ye may prove what is that good, and acceptable, and perfect, will of God.

That is a powerful set of verses. I love reading those, and I know you do too. This is my favorite subject to talk about.

Now let's talk about the law and what it was. My favorite set of verses on the subject are the following.

Galatians 3King James Version (KJV)

3 O foolish Galatians, who hath bewitched you, that ye should not obey the truth, before whose eyes Jesus Christ hath been evidently set forth, crucified among you?

2 This only would I learn of you, Received ye the Spirit by the works of the law, or by the hearing of faith?

3 Are ye so foolish? having begun in the Spirit, are ye now made perfect by the flesh?

4 Have ye suffered so many things in vain? if it be yet in vain.

5 He therefore that ministereth to you the Spirit, and worketh miracles among you, doeth he it by the works of the law, or by the hearing of faith?

6 Even as Abraham believed God, and it was accounted to him for righteousness.

7 Know ye therefore that they which are of faith, the same are the children of Abraham.

8 And the scripture, foreseeing that God would justify the heathen through faith, preached before the gospel unto Abraham, saying, In thee shall all nations be blessed.

9 So then they which be of faith are blessed with faithful Abraham.

10 For as many as are of the works of the law are under the curse: for it is written, Cursed is every one that continueth not in all things which are written in the book of the law to do them.

11 But that no man is justified by the law in the sight of God, it is evident: for, The just shall live by faith.

12 And the law is not of faith: but, The man that doeth them shall live in them.

13 Christ hath redeemed us from the curse of the law, being made a curse for us: for it is written, Cursed is every one that hangeth on a tree:

14 That the blessing of Abraham might come on the Gentiles through Jesus Christ; that we might receive the promise of the Spirit through faith.

15 Brethren, I speak after the manner of men; Though it be but a man's covenant, yet if it be confirmed, no man disannulleth, or addeth thereto.

16 Now to Abraham and his seed were the promises made. He saith not, And to seeds, as of many; but as of one, And to thy seed, which is Christ.

17 And this I say, that the covenant, that was confirmed before of God in Christ, the law, which was four hundred and thirty years after, cannot disannul, that it should make the promise of none effect.

18 For if the inheritance be of the law, it is no more of promise: but God gave it to Abraham by promise.

19 Wherefore then serveth the law? It was added because of transgressions, till the seed should come to whom the promise was made; and it was ordained by angels in the hand of a mediator.

20 Now a mediator is not a mediator of one, but God is one.

21 Is the law then against the promises of God? God forbid: for if there had been a law given which could have given life, verily righteousness should have been by the law.

22 But the scripture hath concluded all under sin, that the promise by faith of Jesus Christ might be given to them that believe.

23 But before faith came, we were kept under the law, shut up unto the faith which should afterwards be revealed.

24 Wherefore the law was our schoolmaster to bring us unto Christ, that we might be justified by faith.

25 But after that faith is come, we are no longer under a schoolmaster.

26 For ye are all the children of God by faith in Christ Jesus.

27 For as many of you as have been baptized into Christ have put on Christ.

28 There is neither Jew nor Greek, there is neither bond nor free, there is neither male nor female: for ye are all one in Christ Jesus.

29 And if ye be Christ's, then are ye Abraham's seed, and heirs according to the promise.

I have preached on that chapter a lot and will probably preach on it many more times before I die. If you have heard me preach in person, I bring it up a lot. I don't think it can be preached enough, to be honest. Paul thought of it enough that this was his main message. Most of his writings involved grace in one way or another. I think even the armor of God consists of the grace of God, but that is another book.

As you can see by the previous verse, the law was only a tutor to lead you to grace. That is all it could do. To get us to see we couldn't do it on our own at all. Like I said before it's impossible to do it on our own. Paul goes as far as to say they were bewitched, thinking they could keep it by the law after they got it by grace. That is something isn't?

Some churches leave that out entirely in their teachings. They correctly preach you get born again by grace, well most preach it, but they preach you have to obey this law and that law to keep your salvation. As you read, that is a lie and isn't biblical at all. You get born-again by grace and keep it by grace.

When I first started preaching, I hated that message. I didn't like the grace message at all, and I was a rather hard preacher. I preached you had to do this; you had to do that. I didn't like to hear grace preachers at all. When God gave me this download, I was completely changed in my message. It's by grace and grace only. Keep reading, and I will fit this all into your identity.

Now that we learned about the law being a tutor and talked some about grace, let's talk about being born-again.

To become a follower of Jesus, you must be born-again.

John 3:3King James Version (KJV)

3 Jesus answered and said unto him, Verily, verily, I say unto thee, Except a man be born again, he cannot see the kingdom of God.

That is in red in the bible, so that means Jesus said it. So, what is being born-again then? Some of you might be born-again and already know this, but I want to go into it anyway. You might fail to see the fullness of this.

Let's first look at the whole chapter of John 3

John 3King James Version (KJV)
3 There was a man of the Pharisees, named Nicodemus, a ruler of the Jews:
2 The same came to Jesus by night, and said unto him, Rabbi, we know that thou art a teacher come from God: for no man can do these miracles that thou doest, except God be with him.
3 Jesus answered and said unto him, Verily, verily, I say unto thee, Except a man be born again, he cannot see the kingdom of God.
4 Nicodemus saith unto him, How can a man be born when he is old? can he enter the second time into his mother's womb, and be born?

5 Jesus answered, Verily, verily, I say unto thee, Except a man be born of water and of the Spirit, he cannot enter into the kingdom of God.

6 That which is born of the flesh is flesh; and that which is born of the Spirit is spirit.

7 Marvel not that I said unto thee, Ye must be born again.

8 The wind bloweth where it listeth, and thou hearest the sound thereof, but canst not tell whence it cometh, and whither it goeth: so is every one that is born of the Spirit.

9 Nicodemus answered and said unto him, How can these things be?

10 Jesus answered and said unto him, Art thou a master of Israel, and knowest not these things?

11 Verily, verily, I say unto thee, We speak that we do know, and testify that we have seen; and ye receive not our witness.

12 If I have told you earthly things, and ye believe not, how shall ye believe, if I tell you of heavenly things?

13 And no man hath ascended up to heaven, but he that came down from heaven, even the Son of man which is in heaven.

14 And as Moses lifted up the serpent in the wilderness, even so must the Son of man be lifted up:

15 That whosoever believeth in him should not perish, but have eternal life.

16 For God so loved the world, that he gave his only begotten Son, that whosoever believeth in him should not perish, but have everlasting life.

17 For God sent not his Son into the world to condemn the world; but that the world through him might be saved.

18 He that believeth on him is not condemned: but he that believeth not is condemned already, because he hath not believed in the name of the only begotten Son of God.

19 And this is the condemnation, that light is come into the world, and men loved darkness rather than light, because their deeds were evil.

20 For every one that doeth evil hateth the light, neither cometh to the light, lest his deeds should be reproved.

21 But he that doeth truth cometh to the light, that his deeds may be made manifest, that they are wrought in God.

22 After these things came Jesus and his disciples into the land of Judaea; and there he tarried with them, and baptized.

23 And John also was baptizing in Aenon near to Salim, because there was much water there: and they came, and were baptized.

24 For John was not yet cast into prison.

25 Then there arose a question between some of John's disciples and the Jews about purifying.

26 And they came unto John, and said unto him, Rabbi, he that was with thee beyond Jordan, to whom thou barest witness, behold, the same baptizeth, and all men come to him.

27 John answered and said, A man can receive nothing, except it be given him from heaven.

28 Ye yourselves bear me witness, that I said, I am not the Christ, but that I am sent before him.

29 He that hath the bride is the bridegroom: but the friend of the bridegroom, which standeth and heareth him, rejoiceth greatly because of the bridegroom's voice: this my joy therefore is fulfilled.

30 He must increase, but I must decrease.

31 He that cometh from above is above all: he that is of the earth is earthly, and speaketh of the earth: he that cometh from heaven is above all.

32 And what he hath seen and heard, that he testifieth; and no man receiveth his testimony.

33 He that hath received his testimony hath set to his seal that God is true.

34 For he whom God hath sent speaketh the words of God: for God giveth not the Spirit by measure unto him.
35 The Father loveth the Son, and hath given all things into his hand.
36 He that believeth on the Son hath everlasting life: and he that believeth not the Son shall not see life; but the wrath of God abideth on him.

Being born-again is being born of the spirit. Nicodemus had a hard time with that at first. He thought it meant being born from your mother twice. Everyone was born the first time from your mother. That was the physical birth. Being born-again is a spiritual birth. Your spirit finally truly comes alive.

Let's look at more verses.

Ephesians 4:23-24 King James Version (KJV)
23 And be renewed in the spirit of your mind;
24 And that ye put on the new man, which after God is created in righteousness and true holiness.

2 Corinthians 5:17 King James Version (KJV)
17 Therefore if any man be in Christ, he is a new creature: old things are passed away; behold, all things are become new.

When you are born-again, you become a new person. You become what God created you to be in the first place. You then become your true self; your true talents come out. You only truly live when you are born-again. That is a powerful thing to think about. Glory

In case you aren't born-again, and you want to be, say,

"Jesus, I need you, help me.
Be the Lord of my life; make me a new person.
Forgive me of my sins."

It doesn't have to be long or hard just from your heart and mean it. That prayer is just an example when Holy Spirit is genuinely on you; you will know what to say. It might just be Jesus, Jesus, Jesus, but that is enough.

Now that I explained being born-again let's talk about the law afterward. I have already talked about the law and explained the law has no power. Well, when you are born-again, you are under grace and not the law. That was talked about in the bible verses I already shared with you a while back, Galatians 3:1-29.

I encourage you to go back and read it. Faith and not the law now justifies you. You are under grace. So now you are a new person. The guilt and sin are washed away. You currently have your real identity.

Remember what I said in the first chapter? About being who you are? Well, that is what I meant by that. I told you it would make sense later on in the book. You can now be who you are because you are now truly made who you are. Now you have the power to be who you are.

Be that writer, that director, musician, songwriter, artist, and be joyful about it. Sanctify those gifts and use them to their fullest now. I will share in another book about the Holy Spirit, what it truly means to be Baptized in the Holy Spirit.

You know, only God can create new things, don't you? The devil can only twist what is already there. Don't believe me? Read the first few chapters in the bible. Let me quote some of it here.

Genesis 1:1-2King James Version (KJV)
1 In the beginning God created the heaven and the earth.
2 And the earth was without form, and void; and darkness was upon the face of the deep. And the Spirit of God moved upon the face of the waters.

There you go, at the first, God created. You see, God was and is the original creator. Now you can tap into that to change the world for the better.

Now let's move on to the next chapter.

Chapter 7
Freedom

John 18:36King James Version (KJV)
36 Jesus answered, My kingdom is not of this world: if my kingdom were of this world, then would my servants fight, that I should not be delivered to the Jews: but now is my kingdom not from hence.

In the last chapter, you learned about what being born-again is. In summary, when you are born-again, you are made a new person and under grace. You are no longer under the law. I gave you several verses talking about it.

In this chapter, you will learn about being sin free. I know it isn't taught like this in most churches and you might be hearing this for the first time. Some teach that you have to strive and work to be free from sin and work for your salvation.

When you are born-again, you are free from works completely. It's not by the works of the law.

> *Romans 11:6King James Version (KJV)*
> *6 And if by grace, then is it no more of works: otherwise grace is no more grace. But if it be of works, then it is no more grace: otherwise work is no more work.*

As you can see by that verse, it's by grace and not by works. I know I have said it in previous chapters, but I can't emphasize it enough.

Let's talk about being free from sin. I will share with you some verses then talk about it.

> *Romans 6:1-14King James Version (KJV)*
> *6 What shall we say then? Shall we continue in sin, that grace may abound?*
> *2 God forbid. How shall we, that are dead to sin, live any longer therein?*
> *3 Know ye not, that so many of us as were baptized into Jesus Christ were baptized into his death?*
> *4 Therefore we are buried with him by baptism into death: that like as Christ was raised up from the dead by the glory of the Father, even so we also should walk in newness of life.*

5 For if we have been planted together in the likeness of his death, we shall be also in the likeness of his resurrection:

6 Knowing this, that our old man is crucified with him, that the body of sin might be destroyed, that henceforth we should not serve sin.

7 For he that is dead is freed from sin.

8 Now if we be dead with Christ, we believe that we shall also live with him:

9 Knowing that Christ being raised from the dead dieth no more; death hath no more dominion over him.

10 For in that he died, he died unto sin once: but in that he liveth, he liveth unto God.

11 Likewise reckon ye also yourselves to be dead indeed unto sin, but alive unto God through Jesus Christ our Lord.

12 Let not sin therefore reign in your mortal body, that ye should obey it in the lusts thereof.

13 Neither yield ye your members as instruments of unrighteousness unto sin: but yield yourselves unto God, as those that are alive from the dead, and your members as instruments of righteousness unto God.

14 For sin shall not have dominion over you: for ye are not under the law, but under grace.

As you can see, when you are born again, you are dead to sin. It doesn't reign in you anymore. I encourage you to read that section of verses over and over because they are powerful.

I know to some that teaching doesn't make any sense and seems like heresy, but as you can see, it's clearly in the bible. You might be saying, "so you are permitting sin?" No, I am not in the slightest.

As you read in Romans 6, Paul addressed that to. People were coming against him and his teaching saying he was condoning sin. They said he was preaching people can do what they wanted. He was preaching just the opposite of it. He was preaching the only real way to be completely free from sin. Not by striving but just being who you are.

Let me put it this way, before being born-again it was about striving. You had to force yourself to live a good life. We all were under the law before being born-again. After being born-again, we are under grace. Grace gives you the power to stay sin free because you are not of this world anymore; you are a part of the kingdom of God. You are born from above, of the spirit you see? You died to sin and are now alive in Jesus.

Here are several Bible verses talking about it.

1 John 2:15-17King James Version (KJV)

15 Love not the world, neither the things that are in the world. If any man love the world, the love of the Father is not in him.
16 For all that is in the world, the lust of the flesh, and the lust of the eyes, and the pride of life, is not of the Father, but is of the world.
17 And the world passeth away, and the lust thereof: but he that doeth the will of God abideth for ever.

John 18:36King James Version (KJV)
36 Jesus answered, My kingdom is not of this world: if my kingdom were of this world, then would my servants fight, that I should not be delivered to the Jews: but now is my kingdom not from hence.

John 15:19King James Version (KJV)
19 If ye were of the world, the world would love his own: but because ye are not of the world, but I have chosen you out of the world, therefore the world hateth you.

So now you don't have to force yourself, you can live it. That is a powerful thing.

If you were a drug addict before being born-again, you are now set free from it. Under the old law, once a drug addict always a drug addict. Well, not when you are born-again, now you are free from it. You aren't that person anymore. You can live a life free from drugs. Glory.

If you were an alcoholic before being born-again, they teach you the same thing. They say "once an alcoholic always one," right? Well, not so, now you are free from that too. You aren't the same person you once were. Glory.

Ephesians 2:9King James Version (KJV)
9 Not of works, lest any man should boast.

As you can see by the previous verse, it isn't by works so that verse proves what I am talking about — another good verse to memorize.

In the next two chapters, I will share with you some tools to stay away from sin, your old person.

Chapter 8
Confessions

Proverbs 18:21King James Version (KJV)
21 Death and life are in the power of the tongue: and
they that love it shall eat the fruit thereof.

J n this chapter, I will discuss confession. This might be a new topic to you, or you heard about it but never thought about it when dealing with your identity. Either way, you are about to learn what confession is and how to use it to step into your identity.

To start, let me share with you a powerful verse and talk about it.

Proverbs 18:21King James Version (KJV)
21 Death and life are in the power of the tongue: and
they that love it shall eat the fruit thereof.

The tongue has power even if you don't want to believe it does, it does. There is a saying that goes something like this, "Sticks and stones may break my bones, but words will never hurt me." Have you ever heard of that saying? I am sure you have. Well, let's talk about that a little bit.

Have you ever had someone always say bad things about you? Do they always say your dumb, fat, or other hurtful things? That hurts doesn't it and affects how you see yourself. It can damage your whole life, to be honest. Those words can stick with you and affect everything you do for maybe your entire life.

Let's say, all the way through grade school people bullied you. They always said horrible things about you and laughed at you. That hurt you more than if you got hit, right? I know it does because I went through that, day after day. It hurts bad. So, the saying about sticks and stones is false, wouldn't you say?

I already shared about being born-again and how you are a new person correct? Sometimes though it's still hard to get over the words that people say. Confession is a powerful tool to use to help get over those words and other things in your life.

Mark 11:23King James Version (KJV)

23 For verily I say unto you, That whosoever shall say unto this mountain, Be thou removed, and be thou cast into the sea; and shall not doubt in his heart, but shall believe that those things which he saith shall come to pass; he shall have whatsoever he saith.

2 Corinthians 10:5King James Version (KJV)
5 Casting down imaginations, and every high thing that exalteth itself against the knowledge of God, and bringing into captivity every thought to the obedience of Christ;

As you can see by the previous two verses, you can take control of your thoughts. At first, it might be hard, but you can. You might ask what does that have to do with a confession. Well, let's look at that.

Let's say you have a thought in your mind to take a drink of alcohol. You immediately say out loud, or under your breath, if you are around people at your job, "I rebuke you bad thought in the name of Jesus." Immediately take control of that thought. If you have to say it several times keep saying it and maybe add, "right now in the name of Jesus." Or" I said right now."

Do that every time you have a lousy thought like that, and eventually, it will be less and less until you finally realize that you don't get them anymore. Wow, that is powerful.

Now let's talk about thoughts that you might have that say you are worthless.

Say these verses out loud.

2 Corinthians 1:20New King James Version (NKJV)
20 For all the promises of God in Him are Yes, and in Him Amen, to the glory of God through us.

2 Corinthians 5:21King James Version (KJV)
21 For he hath made him to be sin for us, who knew no sin; that we might be made the righteousness of God in him.

1 Peter 2:9New International Version (NIV)
9 But you are a chosen people, a royal priesthood, a holy nation, God's special possession, that you may declare the praises of him who called you out of darkness into his wonderful light.

Those are powerful verses, and I encourage you to confess those several times a day every day. It will make a difference in your life, and you will live a life free from the things that hold you back. You will live in your identity and know it. You will be who you are.

You are chosen, your royalty now, your holy, and righteous. That is your identity now because you are born-again. You are made holy because Jesus made you that way not because you earned it by works. That is authentic righteous living and holiness. You can't earn holiness; you are made that way when you are born-again. Glory!

Some teachings say you must do this and do that to be holy. They will tell you; you have to obey the ten commandments and live some laws to be holy. Well, I already shared with you that you are free from the law now. I wonder if they preach that so they can pick and choose the laws you have to obey. It sounds too much like control.

Let's look at a bible verse about where the ten commandments are after you are born again.

Hebrews 10:16King James Version (KJV)

16 This is the covenant that I will make with them after those days, saith the Lord, I will put my laws into their hearts, and in their minds will I write them;

Jeremiah 31:31-35King James Version (KJV)

31 Behold, the days come, saith the Lord, that I will make a new covenant with the house of Israel, and with the house of Judah:

32 Not according to the covenant that I made with their fathers in the day that I took them by the hand to bring them out of the land of Egypt; which my covenant they brake, although I was an husband unto them, saith the Lord:

33 But this shall be the covenant that I will make with the house of Israel; After those days, saith the Lord, I will put my law in their inward parts, and write it in their hearts; and will be their God, and they shall be my people.

34 And they shall teach no more every man his neighbour, and every man his brother, saying, Know the Lord: for they shall all know me, from the least of them unto the greatest of them, saith the Lord: for I will forgive their iniquity, and I will remember their sin no more.

35 Thus saith the Lord, which giveth the sun for a light by day, and the ordinances of the moon and of the stars for a light by night, which divideth the sea when the waves thereof roar; The Lord of hosts is his name:

So, confess that you are righteous, holy, and a saint. Then live it not because you are trying but because that is who you are. Glory.

Chapter 9
Relationship

2 Corinthians 3:18 King James Version (KJV)
18 But we all, with open face beholding as in a glass
the glory of the Lord, are changed into the same image
from glory to glory, even as by the Spirit of the Lord.

There are two types of relationships I want to talk about in this chapter, relationships with God and with people. Both can have an impact on you in a powerful way believe it or not. Let's break this down.

Remember, when I talked about how the longer you are in a relationship with someone, friend, dating, parental, siblings, and family, you become like them? The people you love have influence over you. We are going to talk about that in this chapter in more detail.

Jesus always talked about His relationship with His father. Let me give you some examples with verses in the bible.

John 4:34King James Version (KJV)
34 Jesus saith unto them, My meat is to do the will of him that sent me, and to finish his work.

John 15:9King James Version (KJV)
9 As the Father hath loved me, so have I loved you: continue ye in my love.

John 5:26King James Version (KJV)
26 For as the Father hath life in himself; so hath he given to the Son to have life in himself;

Hebrews 1:3King James Version (KJV)
3 Who being the brightness of his glory, and the express image of his person, and upholding all things by the word of his power, when he had by himself purged our sins, sat down on the right hand of the Majesty on high:

Matthew 6:9King James Version (KJV)
9 After this manner therefore pray ye: Our Father which art in heaven, Hallowed be thy name.

John 8:28King James Version (KJV)

28 Then said Jesus unto them, When ye have lifted up the Son of man, then shall ye know that I am he, and that I do nothing of myself; but as my Father hath taught me, I speak these things.

John 17:8King James Version (KJV)
8 For I have given unto them the words which thou gavest me; and they have received them, and have known surely that I came out from thee, and they have believed that thou didst send me.

Matthew 3:17King James Version (KJV)

17 And lo a voice from heaven, saying, This is my beloved Son, in whom I am well pleased.

Matthew 17:5King James Version (KJV)

5 While he yet spake, behold, a bright cloud overshadowed them: and behold a voice out of the cloud, which said, This is my beloved Son, in whom I am well pleased; hear ye him.

Luke 3:22King James Version (KJV)

22 And the Holy Ghost descended in a bodily shape like a dove upon him, and a voice came from heaven, which said, Thou art my beloved Son; in thee I am well pleased.
2 Peter 1:17King James Version (KJV)

17 For he received from God the Father honour and glory, when there came such a voice to him from the excellent glory, This is my beloved Son, in whom I am well pleased.

I can share with you many more verses about Jesus and His father. The verses I shared shows us many things. He knows what His father is doing; He knows His father, He loves His father and His father loves Him.

So, it's safe to say He had a good relationship with His father. That relationship transformed Him. His father guided Him in everything He did. How much more should we have a relationship with God? He became like His father.

Let's talk about your relationships and how they can have an impact on you. Every person that you are close to and/or around influence you in some way.

Let's say you are in grade school, and others start drinking. The more you are around them, the more likely you are to start drinking too. That happens regularly in America and around the world.

The more you are around your friends, the more you become like them for, the better or worse. If you had a drinking problem in the past and now you are born-again, don't let the people you drank with, influence you anymore. You influence them instead. Become the influencer! Stop letting people have an influence on you for the worse.

This is probably one of the most overlooked things dealing with living a free life and becoming more like God. I am not sure why it's overlooked, maybe it's something people don't want to go into because of fear. Perhaps they don't want to lose the ones they are close to, I am unsure. I am not saying to forget them in whatever relationship you are in with them. I am saying to influence them; to see them live a free life in God. Wouldn't that be great to have more friends to pray with and talk about your experiences with God?

A verse comes to mind just now that I will share with you.

1 Corinthians 7:12-16King James Version (KJV)
12 But to the rest speak I, not the Lord: If any brother hath a wife that believeth not, and she be pleased to dwell with him, let him not put her away.

13 And the woman which hath an husband that believeth not, and if he be pleased to dwell with her, let her not leave him.
14 For the unbelieving husband is sanctified by the wife, and the unbelieving wife is sanctified by the husband: else were your children unclean; but now are they holy.
15 But if the unbelieving depart, let him depart. A brother or a sister is not under bondage in such cases: but God hath called us to peace.
16 For what knowest thou, O wife, whether thou shalt save thy husband? or how knowest thou, O man, whether thou shalt save thy wife?

Notice it didn't say get a divorce it says if they will stay with you stay with them, if they want to get a divorce then let them. What I get out of this verse is, if you can have an influence on them and they let you, please try. Influence them and get them to become a believer. In short, be a witness to them. Live that good life around them and show them how a believer lives. Get them to want to become a believer by showing them how you are. That goes for every relationship you have. Be that witness, not let them change you back to the way you were.

Now let's talk about our relationship with God. Being in God's presence will change you for the better. The more you soak in His presence, the more you become like Him from glory to glory.

2 Corinthians 3:18King James Version (KJV)
18 But we all, with open face beholding as in a glass the glory of the Lord, are changed into the same image from glory to glory, even as by the Spirit of the Lord.

The more you hear Him and see Him, the more you get His heart. The more you want to reach the world. The more you want to see the hurt set free.
Luke 4:18-19King James Version (KJV)
18 The Spirit of the Lord is upon me, because he hath anointed me to preach the gospel to the poor; he hath sent me to heal the brokenhearted, to preach deliverance to the captives, and recovering of sight to the blind, to set at liberty them that are bruised,
19 To preach the acceptable year of the Lord.

Let Him influence you. The more you are in His presence, the more you can be you. I know that might sound strange, but it's very accurate. This is the most important thing a believer can do is be in His presence.

John 10:27King James Version (KJV)
27 My sheep hear my voice, and I know them, and they follow me:

The more you are in His presence, the more you can hear His voice, and you don't want to have Him say, "I never knew you" Do you?

Matthew 7:21-23King James Version (KJV)
21 Not every one that saith unto me, Lord, Lord, shall enter into the kingdom of heaven; but he that doeth the will of my Father which is in heaven.
22 Many will say to me in that day, Lord, Lord, have we not prophesied in thy name? and in thy name have cast out devils? and in thy name done many wonderful works?
23 And then will I profess unto them, I never knew you: depart from me, ye that work iniquity.

Relationships can and will affect you in both good and bad ways. I encourage you to be an influencer and change those around you for the better. Also, let God influence you. So, you can be who you are, a world changer!

Chapter 10
The Dream

W hen I was young, I had this dream from God, and I feel this book is a part of it. I will share with you the dream then how I think knowing your identity is a part of it.

I was looking down at America, and it was dark. The whole country was black with no lights what so ever. All of a sudden, I was standing on the ground and looking at a hill-mountain. It was like it was night and then I was standing on the hill-mountain. I was standing on the very pentacle of it looking north-east. Then what looked like car lights was coming over the mountain then went across the country. I heard a voice that said, "This is the way I am going to come." Then all of a sudden, I was in a room that had a white smooth floor and light was filling the room. It was very bright, but strangely, it didn't hurt my eyes. Then Jesus appeared and asked me a question. "Which way were the lights coming from and going to." I said, "from left to right, from east to west." Jesus said, "don't forget that, whenever you tell people this dream, don't forget to tell them that."

I prayed about that for years and years. I never knew what it meant. Some people said that it was the second coming, but that never felt like the correct explanation to me. A few years ago, God finally told me what it meant. The car lights are people, and they will bring revival all across this country.

You might ask how does this book and identity help with that? Well, knowing your identity will get your light to shine brighter. I pray that every believer's light will shine bright and bring revival to this land.

Let it be so Lord.

America is darker now that it has ever been before, and it's becoming even darker. America needs this now more than ever before. The dream I had is for now, and we need our lights to shine in this darkness. To shed like on this country once again. To see the darkness flee and sin to go. To see the devil run and hide.

We need people to come to Jesus like never before. They need to be changed to their core, and only Jesus can do that. Only He can set them free.

Matthew 5:16King James Version (KJV)
16 Let your light so shine before men, that they may see your good works, and glorify your Father which is in heaven.

ABOUT THE AUTHOR

Chan Smith is a modern day revivalist. He is dedicated to bringing revival to the world and see people set free. He has had many encounters with God starting at an early age setting his life course. He has studied church history, revival history, and the bible thoroughly. He has also had many downloads from God in several biblical subjects that have been confirmed by many. He has had impartations from great revivalist of the modern day. He was commissioned by several pastors from different churches to start his own work that is reaching the world.

Cover designed by Chan Smith

Chan Smith
Visit my website at www.chansmith.org

Printed in the United States of America

Chan Smith Publishing

ISBN - 9781074837358

MORE FROM AUTHOR

Holy Spirit and Fire
Healing is for You

Your Identity

Notes

Your Identity

Chan Smith

Your Identity

Chan Smith

Chan Smith

Made in the USA
Columbia, SC
21 February 2023

12703542R00117